The Master Musicians Series

SIBELIUS

SERIES EDITED BY

SIR JACK WESTRUP

M.A., Hon. D.Mus.(Oxon.), F.R.C.O.

VOLUMES IN THE
MASTER MUSICIANS SERIES

Composer	Author
Bach	Eva Mary and Sydney Grew
Beethoven	Marion M. Scott
Berlioz	J. H. Elliot
Brahms	Peter Latham
Bruckner and Mahler	H. F. Redlich
Chopin	Arthur Hedley
Debussy	Edward Lockspeiser
Dvořák	Alec Robertson
Gluck	Alfred Einstein
Handel	Percy M. Young
Haydn	Rosemary Hughes
Liszt	Walter Beckett
Mendelssohn	Philip Radcliffe
Monteverdi	Denis Arnold
Mozart	Eric Blom
Mussorgsky	M. D. Calvocoressi
Palestrina	Henry Coates
Purcell	Sir Jack Westrup
Ravel	Norman Demuth
Schubert	Arthur Hutchings
Schumann	Joan Chissell
Sibelius	Robert Layton
Tchaikovsky	Edwin Evans
Vaughan Williams	James Day
Verdi	Dyneley Hussey
Wagner	Robert L. Jacobs

In preparation

Composer	Author
Elgar	Diana McVeagh

Photo: Bertil Dahlgren

SIBELIUS IN 1954

THE MASTER MUSICIANS SERIES

SIBELIUS

by

ROBERT LAYTON

With eight pages of plates and music examples in the text

LONDON
J. M. DENT AND SONS LTD

FARRAR, STRAUS AND GIROUX, INC.
NEW YORK

Made in Great Britain
at the
Aldine Press · Letchworth · Herts
for
J. M. DENT & SONS LTD
Aldine House · Bedford Street · London
First published 1965

To D. C. B. P.

The deeper a man's solitude the more powerful his language . . .

Hofmannsthal (Book of Friends)

PREFACE

When in 1947 Gerald Abraham's symposium on Sibelius first appeared, the critical climate differed a good deal from the present time. The Sibelius 'cult' which Gray's books and Constant Lambert's *Music Ho!* had helped to foster was still at its height, and it was only in the mid fifties that signs of a reaction began to show. To a certain extent the reaction is that of a younger generation of critics against the critical Establishment of the day, and as much a protest against their sins of omission as anything else. Such a reaction was as inevitable as it will be temporary.

It was an encounter with some unfamiliar Sibelius that rekindled my childhood love of the composer, and in returning to him in the late fifties I found my admiration for the familiar seven symphonies increasing by leaps and bounds while the exploration of less familiar terrain proved no less exciting an experience. I have attempted in this short volume to represent the findings of other writers as well; Abraham, Parmet, Rosas and Wood are authorities whose writings have a different brief from those in the Master Musicians series but whose ideas cannot be ignored. For the chronological list of works I have drawn on such authorities as Solanterä (1955), Johnson (1959) and Tanzberger (1962), as well as subsequent discoveries and personal inquiry. I am indebted to Mr Arre Hemming for information about writings in Finnish that help to make the bibliography reasonably comprehensive.

I owe a special debt of gratitude to Mr John Rosas of the Sibelius Museum, Turku, on whose admirable researches I have drawn in the chapter devoted to Sibelius's early chamber works. To Mrs Alfhild Forslin of the Turku Museum, to Mrs Eva Palohaimo, the composer's eldest daughter, I am indebted for numerous kindnesses. Thanks are also due to Sir Jack Westrup for his editorial suggestions and to Mr Peter Branscombe and Mr David Palmer for their assistance in reading the book in proof. Finally warm thanks to Mr Terry Homans of the Goldhurst Foundation for preparing an index and to the Fellows of Corpus Calthorpe College for their encouragement.

R. L.

London,
June 1965.

CONTENTS

ILLUSTRATIONS

CHAPTER I

THE EARLY YEARS

FEW great composers have equalled Sibelius in terms of longevity. Verdi and Vaughan Williams come nearest, though neither attained his ninetieth year: among writers, Shaw surpassed him by only a couple of years. No other composer has witnessed so great a change in the language of music during his lifetime. When Sibelius was born, Berlioz was still alive and Liszt in his fifties; the deaths of Chopin, Mendelssohn and Schumann were as recent as those of Bartók, Schönberg and Prokofiev are in the 1960's. Berlioz's music was as modern then as Bartók's is now. Much of the music that has since passed into the standard repertory, including that of Tchaikovsky, Dvořák and Brahms, was 'contemporary music', and while Sibelius was a young man, Richard Strauss was the young revolutionary. At his death in 1957 the language of music was transformed out of all recognition: Mahler, Debussy, *Les Six*, Berg, to take only a few names at random, had set their stamp on the expressive means at the composer's disposal; Webern was in the process of assimilation by the rising generation, Nono and Boulez were beginning to emerge among the leading *avant-garde* composers, while Stravinsky was, as usual, leaving them all gnawing at the post.

Such far-reaching changes are not confined to music. No period has ever seen such an enormously accelerated rate of technological progress as the present century; and the political structure of Europe has changed in a way that few could have imagined in 1865. In the year of Sibelius's birth Finland was a backwater, a smallish province on the north-western perimeter of Tsarist Russia, a country that had itself abolished serfdom only four years earlier.

Throughout the eighteenth century Finland remained Swedish; but in 1809 she changed her Swedish rulers for Russian tutelage, and from that time until the Russian revolution was an autonomous duchy of the Tsarist empire. For the most part the day-to-day administration of the country's affairs remained in the hands of the Swedish-speaking civil service. Swedish was the language of the educated classes, for most were descendants of Swedes who had emigrated to Finland during the *Storhetstiden*, while Finnish, spoken by the large majority of the people, enjoyed a subservient status. Many Finns never mastered both tongues; formal education, as well as the business of government, was conducted in Swedish, but as the movement for self-determination gathered impetus during the course of the nineteenth century, so Finnish began to assert itself as a cultural force.

It was into a Swedish-speaking home that the young Sibelius was born on 8th December 1865. He was the second of three children: the eldest was a girl, Linda, born two years earlier, and the youngest a boy called Christian. Their father was a doctor attached to the military garrison at Hämeenlinna (Tavastehus),[1] a small town in south-central Finland; and his wife, Maria Christina, also came from a Swedish-speaking family in whose veins the blood of clergymen, government officials, landowners and other members of the professional classes freely mingled. The surname itself seems to have come into being during the eighteenth century, when Johan Martinpoika, a farmer from Artjävi (Artsjö) in central Finland (and the composer's great-grandfather on the paternal side), had moved south to Lapinjärvi (Lappträsk), where he took the name 'Sibbe' from the plot of land that he farmed. It is clear that the Latinized form of the name soon came to be adopted. His son, Johan (Sibelius's grandfather), moved to Loviisa, a coastal town to the east of Helsinki: here he was active as a business man and town councillor. He subsequently married Catharina Fredrika, the daughter of a Swedish doctor, Mathias Åkerberg, who had emigrated from Skåne. Both she and her son, Christian Gustaf (Sibelius's father) were musical.[2]

[1] Swedish place-names are given in brackets.

[2] In his biography of Sibelius published in 1931 Cecil Gray declared that 'of the thirty-two direct ancestors of Sibelius living about 1700, eighteen were Finnish Swedes—i.e. persons of Swedish origin living in Finland—nine were pure Swedes, and one was German, leaving only four pure Finns'. He then went on to conclude that 'Sibelius is predominantly,

SIBELIUS AS A BOY OF ELEVEN

Christian Gustaf and his young wife gave their first son the names Johan Julius Christian, the first presumably to honour the memory of his grandfather or that of his uncle, Christian's eldest brother, who had died in Havana two years before Janne's birth. The boy was always called Janne by his relatives and friends rather than Johan or Jan. He acquired the Christian name by which he is universally known from his widely travelled uncle Johan, who was a sea captain: his uncle used the French form of his name when abroad (a not uncommon practice at that time), and the discovery some twenty years later of a bunch of visiting-cards bearing the name Jean Sibelius prompted Janne to follow his uncle's example.

Janne's father died of typhus during the epidemic of 1867 when the boy was only two and a half, and Maria Christina a mere twenty-seven. Not unnaturally the young mother returned to her own home in Hämeenlinna, and Janne spent most of his childhood winters there in his grandmother's home. His summers, which he spent with his paternal grandmother at Loviisa, gave rise to an early and enduring love of nature. Since both his grandmothers were widows Janne was deprived of masculine influence during the formative years, though he was deeply attached to his uncle Pehr, a keen amateur musician and astronomer, who had a highly successful business in Turku (Åbo), Finland's leading seaport on the south-west coast.

Apart from the loss of his father, these early years were happy ones: Maria Christina was a devoted and loving mother who inspired the deepest affection in her family, and Janne seems in every way to have enjoyed a normal, healthy childhood. Although he displayed every evidence of musical talent he was by no means a prodigy, and his family did not envisage a musical career for him. However, his musical interests were encouraged as were those of the other children. Linda learned the piano and Christian the cello: Janne himself began piano

---

even overwhelmingly, Swedish, not Finnish'. This is a highly misleading statement, since the Swedish-speaking Finns possess a distinctive and highly developed culture which is purely Finnish. To describe Sibelius as Swedish is as inaccurate as calling a French-speaking Canadian a Frenchman.

lessons at the age of nine, but it soon became clear that his heart lay with the violin. It was not until he was in his fifteenth year that he began to study the violin in earnest with Gustav Levander, who was bandmaster at Hämeenlinna. He entertained ambitions of becoming a virtuoso for some time and studied with great zeal and enthusiasm. It was no doubt a bitter disappointment for him when he realized in his early twenties that he had embarked on the violin at too late an age for him to achieve complete mastery of his chosen instrument.

As a schoolboy he practised energetically—to the detriment of his normal schooling. The latter began at the age of eight, when he entered a Swedish-language elementary school; this he subsequently left in order to acquire enough Finnish for him to enter the Hämeenlinna *Suomalainen Normaalilyseo* (Tavastehus *Finska Normallyceum*), one of the very first Finnish-language schools. Janne did not excel academically; he was for the most part bored with the usual academic drill, though he was an avid reader even at that age, devouring among other things a good deal of classical literature and Swedish poetry. One of his school friends, Walter von Konow, has given a charming portrait of Janne as a child: he has described him as something of a dreamer, and testified to his passionate love of nature, his extraordinarily vivid fantasy, and his sudden changes of mood from a playful exuberance to the deepest melancholy. He seems to have been a spontaneous child, easily moved and with an affectionate nature.

He had already begun to compose: a little piece called *Vattendroppar* (*Water Drops*), for violin and cello *pizzicato*, dates from 1875 when he was in his tenth year. The urge to compose became irresistible, and in 1881, when he was fifteen, he pored over Marx's composition treatise and became quite a prolific composer of chamber music. These years include the A minor piano trio and the piano quartet in E minor (both written in 1881–2), a violin sonata, written the same year, the *Andantino* for cello and piano (1884), and a large amount of other chamber and instrumental music besides. These he naturally wrote for use at home and played them together with his brother and sister: the family also explored the classical repertory—Haydn, Mozart and Beethoven—as well as the Romantics, including Grieg and other Scandinavian composers. So absorbed was Janne in music-making and composition that he neglected his school work during the crucial years before the *studentexam*, the advanced school-leaving examination that qualifies for entrance into the university. However, after some months of assiduous application to the school curriculum, he finally gained his *studenten* in May 1885, when he was nineteen.

His family, and in particular his grandmother, Catharina Juliana Borg, considered music too precarious a career for him, and that autumn he began his law studies at the university of Helsinki. At the same time, armed with a recently completed string quartet in E flat, he enrolled as a part-time student at the conservatoire, taking courses in both violin and harmony and counterpoint. His musical studies tended to absorb most of his energies, and Sibelius himself told his biographer, Karl Ekman, how when one of his uncles who taught at a provincial school paid a surprise visit to him in Helsinki, he discovered Janne's textbooks untouched, while musical activity, on the other hand, was greatly in evidence. The family wisely bowed to the inevitable, and when the next academic year began Janne was allowed to devote his whole time to music.

At the conservatoire, which was then under the enlightened direction of Martin Wegelius, Sibelius's first teacher had been the Hungarian, Csillag, but when he became a full-time student in his second year in Helsinki, Wegelius himself took a great interest in the youth and they became fast friends. Janne spent many weeks at Wegelius's summer house studying counterpoint with him in the mornings, playing violin sonatas during the afternoon and relaxing over a bottle of wine during the evening. Wegelius's enthusiasms infected most of his pupils: he was an ardent Wagnerite, and consequently works of Brahms seldom appeared in any of the conservatoire's concerts. Janne continued to compose profusely: another violin sonata dates from his first year in Helsinki, and was followed by the so-called Korpo trio. This work derives its name from the small estate where Sibelius wrote the work during the summer of 1887. Three of his student works from this period find their inspiration in literary sources: *Trånaden* (*Longing*) for piano, to accompany verses by Stagnelius, *Svartsjukans nätter* (*Nights of Jealousy*) to accompany the declamation of a poem of Runeberg, and thirdly, two songs for Gunnar Wennerberg's fairy-tale drama *Näcken* (*The Watersprite*). These were written for a production of the play in the spring of 1888 for which Wegelius wrote the bulk of the music. It is a measure of the esteem in which he held his young pupil that Wegelius asked Janne to provide two of the vocal numbers of the play. Later in the same spring, on 31st May, his Theme and Variations in C sharp minor for string quartet were first given at a concert at the conservatoire: these received the blessing of no less a person than Karl Flodin, the most influential Finnish critic of the day.

Janne had not entirely abandoned hope of becoming a violin virtuoso, and continued to play a great deal. He was evidently a fine violinist, since he had already been appointed second violin in the conservatoire's official string quartet in 1887, and pianists like Wegelius and Faltin, the high priests of Finnish musical life, were not ashamed to accompany him. But composition continued to make further inroads on his time and energies. In his last term as a student in the spring of 1889 he produced two new works, a suite in A for string trio (13th April), and a string quartet in A minor (29th May). Flodin hailed the quartet enthusiastically:

> In this work Mr Sibelius has given such striking proof of his original musical talent that one can expect great things of him. In all the different movements of the quartet there emerges a fertility of invention and an independence, combined with a mastery of technique, that must be regarded as unique in so young a composer. Mr Sibelius has with one stroke placed himself foremost amongst those who have been entrusted with bearing the banner of Finnish music.[1]

Flodin was not the only one in whom Janne's creative gifts evoked a warm response. While he was still a student, Busoni joined the staff as piano professor, and a close and enduring friendship grew up

[1] Hr Sibelius har i och med denna komposition avgivit ett så lysande prov på originell musikalisk begåvning, att man bör kunna vänta det största av honom. I alla de olika satserna av kvartetten framträdde en idérikedom och självständighet, parade med herravälde över de tekniska svårigheterna, som måste betecknas såsom unika egenskaper hos en så ung tonsättare. Hr Sibelius har med ett slag ställt sig i första ledet av dem, åt vilka det blivit anförtrott att föra den finska skapande tonkonstens runor.

between the two young men. They both spent a good deal of time together at various Helsinki cafés and restaurants, their conversation ranging over a wide field of topics. Busoni was to show in practical form his admiration of Sibelius's art when he later introduced some of his work to continental audiences. He dedicated the first movement of his *Geharnischte* Suite to Sibelius, the last two movements being inscribed to the Järnefelt brothers.

These years in Helsinki brought Janne into contact with most of the leading figures in Finnish cultural life, including Adolf Paul, a young pianist and writer, as well as the Järnefelt family into which Sibelius was soon to marry. His gifts had been widely acclaimed, and by means of a state scholarship supplemented by fifteen hundred Finnmarks from the Nyland *Kiseleffska* stipendium he was enabled to continue his studies on the Continent.

CHAPTER II

1889–1897

ON 7th September 1889 Wegelius waved farewell to his gifted pupil, who set sail for Lübeck on the first stage of his visit to Germany. Sibelius spent the first year of his period on the Continent in Berlin, which naturally made a considerable impact on him. Helsinki was a small provincial town at this time: Berlin was Sibelius's first taste of life in a musical centre of real importance. He studied there with Albert Becker, a strict academic of the old school, and produced the usual abundance of fugues and exercises in vocal and instrumental counterpoint. But it was the vast amount of music that he heard in Berlin, rather than Becker's teaching, that made the greatest impression on him. Here he was able to hear a much more extensive orchestral repertory than Helsinki could offer: Hans von Bülow conducted the Philharmonic Orchestra's concerts, and Strauss's *Don Juan* was among the novelties of the season. Joachim's performances of the late Beethoven quartets at the *Königliche Hochschule* were a revelation to him, as were von Bülow's recitals of Beethoven's piano sonatas.

Strangely enough, one of the novelties of the season to make the greatest impression on Sibelius was a Finnish work, the *Aino* symphony of Robert Kajanus, who conducted its first performance in Berlin with the Philharmonic Orchestra. Sibelius took the opportunity of making the acquaintance of his fellow countryman, who was later to become one of the finest exponents of his music.[1] The *Aino* symphony opened Sibelius's eyes to the wonderful possibilities which the *Kalevala* offered for musical expression. Under Becker's

[1] Kajanus had founded the Helsinki Orchestral Society in 1882, but relations between him and Wegelius were somewhat strained, so that Sibelius had not been actively encouraged to visit Kajanus's concerts as a student, though in fact he did on occasion do so.

SIBELIUS'S BIRTHPLACE

strict guidance Sibelius ploughed the furrows of academic counterpoint and completed only one original work during his year in Berlin, the piano quintet in G minor. He had still to embark on an orchestral piece, though he had for some time during his student years planned a *Macbeth* symphony.

After a short visit to Busoni in Leipzig in the spring of 1890, Sibelius returned to Finland, where he spent a great deal of the summer with the Järnefelt family; in the autumn he became engaged to their daughter Aino. He remained in Finland long enough to hear the first public performance on 13th October of his string quartet in B flat (Op. 4), which he had written shortly before his departure for Berlin the previous year.

A few days later he left for Vienna, where he was to spend the next year, armed with a letter of introduction to Brahms, written by his friend Busoni. Brahms, whose rudeness to people in general and young composers in particular was legendary, refused to see him, though they did eventually meet accidentally at the Leidinger café. Sibelius studied in Vienna, however, with two of its leading figures, Robert Fuchs (whom he met through the good offices of Hans Richter) and Karl Goldmark, who was at the height of his powers at this time. Certainly these months were more productive than the Berlin period; apart from a piano quartet in C major and a fair number of songs, three of which he later included in his first song cycle, the seven Runeberg settings, Op. 13, he took his first steps into the realms of orchestral music with an overture in E major, which was first performed in Helsinki later the same spring. From these months too come the sketches for an octet for flute, clarinet and strings that were to provide the material for *En Saga*.

Sibelius returned from Vienna in the summer of 1891, greatly stimulated by his visit. The remainder of the year he spent in Loviisa with his family, working on the projects that he had begun on the Continent, including the *Kullervo* symphony. This, his first major work to draw on the *Kalevala* for its inspiration, was an enormous success at its first performance on 28th April 1892. The work is of generous proportions and calls for large forces, including two soloists, chorus and orchestra, and plays for eighty minutes. It was regarded as a landmark in Finnish music at the time, and reflected the increasing national self-consciousness that was a feature of the period. The nineties saw a hardening of Russia's grip on Finland, and Sibelius's friendship with the group of nationalist writers, including Juhani Aho and Arvid Järnefelt, and his sympathy for the aims of their paper, *Päivälehti*, was well known. The success of *Kullervo* was so resounding that it would have dispelled any doubts (had there ever been any) that the Järnefelt family may have entertained about marrying their daughter to a musician; for with his marriage to Aino on 10th June Sibelius entered one of the most prominent and aristocratic of the Finnish-speaking families.

After a short honeymoon in the Karelia, Sibelius returned to take up the two part-time teaching appointments he had been offered, one at Kajanus's orchestral school and the other at Wegelius's conservatoire. With the success of *Kullervo* fresh in his mind, Kajanus asked him for an orchestral work for the coming season, and the outcome of this was *En Saga*, which Sibelius himself conducted at its *première* on 16th February 1893. It was not, however, the popular piece that Kajanus had expected, and did not meet with wide critical acclamation; it was subsequently withdrawn for revision, and the version we know today dates from 1901.

Though *En Saga* has no programme, Sibelius turned for his next work to the *Kalevala*. This was an opera, *Veneen luominen* (*The Building of the Boat*), for which *The Swan of Tuonela* was originally intended as a prelude. It was his work on this opera, which he abandoned in the autumn of the same year, that gave him the idea for the *Four Legends* which comprise the *Lemminkäinen Suite*. With *The Swan* already complete, Sibelius laid aside all his other summer work in order to fulfil a commission from the Viipuri Student Association for incidental music to a series of historical tableaux which were first given on 13th November. From this material he drew up his *Karelia* music, an overture, Op. 10, and the better-known suite, Op. 11. These months also saw the completion of *Vårsång* (*Song of Spring*), first performed on 21st June 1894 as *Impromptu for Orchestra*, a good deal of piano music, and songs, including the glorious setting of Runeberg's *Se'n har jag ej frågat mera (Since then I have questioned no further).*

Composition of the 'Four Legends'

It was in the summer of 1894 that Sibelius made the first of his many visits to Italy, a land which he greatly loved. On the way home his brother-in-law, Armas Järnefelt, inveigled him into visiting Bayreuth, though he never succeeded in turning him into a Wagnerite. Throughout this time Sibelius was still working on the remaining three legends of the *Lemminkäinen* suite, which had occupied him in fact since the completion of *The Swan* in the summer of 1893. They were eventually finished at the end of 1895 and first heard the following year, though, as with the case of *En Saga,* they were subjected to further revisions, the first being in 1897 for another public performance. One interesting curiosity from these years is Sibelius's only opera, a one-act piece called *Jungfrun i tornet* (*The Maiden in the Tower*) to a text of Rafael Herzberg. This was actually performed (7th November 1896), though in common with the occasional works Sibelius produced at the time—the cantatas written for the university ceremonies of 1894 and the coronation of Nicolas II two years later—it remained in manuscript.

At this juncture, when Sibelius had yet to compose his first symphony, an important token of recognition came his way. This was the award of a State pension, an enlightened gesture on the part of the Finnish Senate, though the sum granted, 3,000 Finnish marks, did not free him from all financial worries. He continued his teaching activities, though on a smaller scale than before, and later undertook several concert tours to supplement his income. Sibelius was not a good business man, and often sold his works to publishers on disadvantageous terms: he often signed away the rights of mechanical reproduction which would have been the source of considerable royalties. Nevertheless the State pension did guarantee him a minimum income, and reflected the tremendous faith of the Finns in their young composer.

CHAPTER III

1898–1918

THE last years of the nineteenth century were busy ones for Sibelius: the music for Adolf Paul's *King Christian II* (1898) and the six songs, Op. 36, which include his best-known song, *Svarta Rosor* (*Black Roses*), date from this time. However, his most important work was the first symphony. Sibelius had for long felt the urge to compose an entirely orchestral symphony: the influential Flodin himself, in a review hailing a symphony by a much younger Finn, Ernst Mielck, made a clear hint that he should take up the symphonic challenge, and Sibelius was not slow in responding. Work on the first symphony occupied him during the latter part of 1898 and the spring of 1899, its first performance taking place on 28th April that year under the composer's direction.

But 1899 was a period of considerable political unrest in Finland, and Sibelius was caught up in the mounting fever of nationalism. This was occasioned by a number of repressive measures taken by the Russians in the so-called February Manifesto, which deprived Finland of her autonomy and drastically curtailed the freedom of speech and assembly that the Finns had hitherto enjoyed. Sibelius responded with a quantity of patriotic music, including a setting of Rydberg's *Aternarnas Sång* and a series of tableaux for the celebrations in November in aid of the Press Pension Fund, a seemingly harmless event which was, however, laden with political fervour and assumed something of the character of a patriotic demonstration. Kajanus subsequently conducted four of these tableaux, the first three being what we now know as the *Scènes historiques I*, Op. 25, and the last being *Finland Awakes*, to which Sibelius gave the title *Finlandia* when he revised it the following year.

Sibelius's reputation was at this time beginning to grow abroad. While he was in Germany in 1898 Adolf Paul introduced him to

Breitkopf & Härtel in Leipzig, who became his continental publishers. Two years later the Finnish Orchestra under Kajanus visited Scandinavia and the Continent to take part in the Paris Exhibition of 1900, and Sibelius's music figured prominently on their programmes. One of the planners of this tour had been Axel Carpelan, who became one of Sibelius's firmest friends. It was Carpelan who placed sufficient funds at his disposal to enable him to give up teaching for a year and take his family abroad. He stayed for some weeks in Berlin before going to Italy, where he wintered. In May he returned to Germany by way of Prague, where he met Suk, whose acquaintance he had previously made in Berlin, and Dvořák, who made a great impression on him. In Germany he conducted two of the *Lemminkäinen Legends* at the Heidelberg Festival in the latter part of June 1901, before retracing his steps to Italy. During the autumn of that year and the winter of 1902 he lived in Italy, renting a villa at Rapallo, where he composed the second symphony and revised *En Saga.* The symphony he dedicated to Carpelan as a gesture of gratitude for his year in Italy. It was finished early in 1902 and Sibelius himself directed its first performance in Helsinki in March.

He followed it up with the choral work *The Origin of Fire* (*Ukko the Firemaker*), first given a month later for the inauguration of the Finnish National Theatre. Janne spent the remainder of the summer in the Finnish countryside and returned to Helsinki in the autumn. Some of his finest songs, the Op. 38 set, including *Autumn Evening*, date from this time. Early the following year he wrote his incidental music for Arvid Järnefelt's *Kuolema* (*Death*), and he must have often regretted selling the famous *Valse triste* from this score for an outright sum to his Helsinki publisher. In doing so he signed away a small fortune in royalties: it was arranged for all sorts of combinations and played in every café in Europe and America during the pre-war era, sharing the fate which befell *Finlandia.* The violin concerto was also begun in 1903 and finished the same summer. It was first heard on 8th February the following year with Viktor Nováček as soloist, but the composer was again unhappy about it and it was revised. In its definitive form it was given in Berlin in 1905 with Richard Strauss conducting.

In 1904 Sibelius decided to leave Helsinki and live in the country. He told Rosa Newmarch some years later: 'Give me the loneliness either of the Finnish forests or of a big city'; and he certainly seems to have worked better in the depths of the Finnish countryside than in Helsinki. The latter offered too many social distractions, and Sibelius was fond of the luxuries of good living. London, Paris or Berlin were another matter, for there he could escape into the solitude of the great city. His choice fell on the little village of Järvenpää (Träskända) about 35 kilometres north-east of Helsinki, where the writer Aho had also chosen to live. Its close proximity to Helsinki enabled him to make frequent trips to the capital. He named his villa *Ainola* after his wife; and here in the closing weeks of 1904 he embarked on the sketches of a third symphony.

The same autumn he received an invitation to visit England, which he planned to do after his journey to Berlin in January 1905 to conduct the German *première* of his second symphony at one of Busoni's New Music concerts. In the meantime, however, he was commissioned to write incidental music to Maeterlinck's *Pelléas et Mélisande* for a production in Bertil Gripenberg's translation at the Swedish Theatre in Helsinki. This compelled him to postpone his English trip until November. His music was now beginning to make encouraging progress abroad: Toscanini included some of his works in his concerts in Milan, and in England, since Henry Wood introduced the *King Christian* music to the Promenade Concerts in 1901, he was gradually gaining ground. Bantock had conducted the first symphony in March 1905 and Hans Richter gave the second its English *première* at a Hallé concert during the same year.

England seems to have appealed to Sibelius, and he was so liberally entertained by Bantock that he 'never made the acquaintance of English coinage'. After conducting in the north he came to London, where he met Henry Wood and promised to conduct the *première* of his new symphony in February 1907. He continued to work on it while he was in Paris, where his music was also making limited headway: three years earlier he had received the *Légion d'honneur* from the French authorities. In January 1906 he returned home and immersed himself in composition: the third symphony, incidental music to *Belshazzar's*

Feast by his friend Hjalmar Procopé, and the symphonic poem *Pohjola's Daughter*, which he completed later that year and first gave at a concert in St Petersburg in December the same year.

The new symphony was not in fact completed until the following year. So slow was its progress that the *première* which had been promised to the Royal Philharmonic Society for March 1907 had to be postponed. The composer eventually conducted it in February 1908 and paid Bantock the compliment of dedicating it to him. During this second London visit Sibelius was increasingly troubled by severe pains in the throat, which he suspected to be the result of a cancerous growth. This cast a dark shadow over his life at this time, for he was at the height of his creative powers and saddled with family responsibilities. After two operations a malignant tumour was successfully removed and he was sufficiently recovered in health to make a return journey to England in the winter of 1909, though he was forced to abjure cigars and alcohol. He met a number of important figures in English musical life, including Bax and Goossens, and also such illustrious visitors to London as d'Indy and Debussy: he heard the latter's *Nocturnes*, Elgar's first symphony, Bantock's *Omar Khayyam*, and a large quantity of other contemporary music. He conducted a number of his own works, including *En Saga*, and did a good deal of composition; it was at the end of his visit in March that he completed the quartet *Voces intimae*, which he had begun the previous December. Nor were the following months idle: 1909 saw the first performance of *Nightride and Sunrise*, one of his most neglected tone-poems, the completion of *In Memoriam*, the Op. 57 songs and the charming settings of two lyrics from Shakespeare's *Twelfth Night*. Sibelius also took the opportunity of drawing up an orchestral suite from the music he had written the previous year for the Swedish Theatre's production of Strindberg's *Swanwhite*.

In the spring of 1910 he began work on his fourth symphony, and this occupied him throughout the year, which was a troubled one in Finland, since Russian attempts to subdue the rising nationalist feeling were intensified. Sibelius took the symphony with him on his travels and worked on it when he visited Oslo in the autumn (where he conducted a newly completed tone poem, *The Dryad*), then continued with it in Berlin and Leipzig. Early in the new year he made another concert tour embracing Sweden and the Baltic states, presenting his new symphony on his return home. It received its *première* in Helsinki on 3rd April 1911, in a programme devoted entirely to his most recent music, and it did not fail to puzzle the audience. Reaction abroad was equally bewildered; in Gothenburg the work was hissed and in America it was roundly abused as 'ultra-modern' and 'dissonant and doleful'. Its reception in this country was a little more sympathetic: Sibelius himself conducted it on his visit in the autumn of 1912, when it formed the main work on the programmes that he gave in Liverpool, Manchester, Bournemouth and Birmingham, where Bantock had succeeded Elgar as professor of music. Early the same year he received another token of the esteem in which he was held abroad: the Imperial Music Academy of Vienna offered him a post as professor of composition. He declined this, as he was to decline most foreign offers of a similar nature, though during the weeks in which he made up his mind pressure was brought on the Finnish Senate to increase his State pension from 3,000 to 5,000 Finnish marks.

Sibelius continued to travel widely: the autumn of 1911 he spent in Berlin, where he heard an enormous quantity of music. He had promised at the end of his last English visit to return and conduct a new choral work in Gloucester Cathedral in 1913; he also wrote to Rosa Newmarch that he was planning a longer visit to this country as a tourist. However, he never completed the choral work in time and hence felt unable to make the trip; though by way of atonement *Luonnotar*, one of his most elusive pieces, probably composed about 1910, was given to Gloucester for its first performance, which took place in September 1913; that year also saw the composition of one of his finest and most rarely heard masterpieces, the tone-poem *The Bard.*

The same year he received, and at first declined, an invitation to visit America; he eventually accepted in August 1913 and began to plan the commission he had received with it from Norfolk, Connecticut. The original plan was that he should write a choral work for the Norfolk Festival, but this subsequently turned out to be the purely

SIBELIUS AT THIRTY

orchestral tone-poem *The Oceanides.* He began the first version of this in Berlin in January 1914, completing it on his return to Järvenpää. He arrived in New York on his long-planned visit in May 1914, having rewritten *The Oceanides,* which he conducted at Norfolk on 4th June. He was the guest of Carl Stoeckel, an American patron of the arts, and received the warmest of welcomes. Sibelius's music had figured on concert programmes as abundantly in America as it had in England: the composer found himself more famous than he had imagined. He was given an honorary degree [1] at Yale; he was lavishly entertained by his American hosts, widely dined (though not wined, for since his illness he was compelled to exercise some restraint in this direction), and a chance remark dropped by the composer even prompted his host to indulge him to the extent of giving him the daily attentions of a private barber to carry out his morning shave. Sibelius was delighted by it all, and even toyed with plans to return for a concert tour. He wrote to his brother Christian: 'I think that a planned tour of forty to fifty concerts would succeed. Then I could pay off both your debts and my own.' However, the outbreak of the First World War in the following month put an end to these and many other plans he had made.

Sibelius did not long escape the consequences of the war. Breitkopf & Härtel had for long been a major source of revenue for him, since Finland did not adhere to the Berne convention on copyright. Breitkopf's catalogue of Sibelius's music ran to no fewer than twenty-three pages, and an energetic advertising campaign resulted in performances of his work all over Europe and America (and even as far away as Shanghai). With the outbreak of war the connection with Breitkopf became more difficult and eventually lapsed, and Sibelius began his association with the famous Danish publishing house of Hansen. We find him during these dark and difficult years writing a much higher proportion of small piano pieces, songs and other miniatures, and there is no doubt that commercial considerations may have prompted this. However, he started work on a fifth symphony not long after the war began, and finished it in time for his fiftieth

[1] The Alexander University of Helsinki also conferred the same honour on him at this time, though *in absentia.*

birthday the following year. The event was treated almost as a national holiday: speeches, telegrams, greetings and gifts were showered on the shy composer. A few months later he received an honour from the Tsar, who gave him the title of professor the following spring.

The fifth symphony still troubled Sibelius, even after its successful *première*: it was subjected to two revisions, the first in 1916 and the second three years later. The collection of piano miniatures, Op. 74, 75 and 76, similar sets of violin pieces, Op. 79 and 81, and the sonatina, Op. 80, all date from the period 1914–15. But, apart from miniatures such as these and the songs, Op. 86 and 90, it is the fifth symphony which dominated the war years.

Although Finland was not the scene of hostilities during the earlier part of the war, the outbreak of the Russian Revolution in 1917 had immediate repercussions. To forestall a left-wing rising the middle classes in Finland organized themselves into military cadres which became known as the White Guard; the Social Democrats and the left-wing groups were not slow to follow suit. A month after the October Revolution, when the Bolsheviks seized the reins of government, Finland proclaimed her independence. In January 1918, however, the Red Guards attempted a *coup d'état* and Finland was plunged into civil war. Sibelius was in some peril, since his sympathies were known to be with the Whites. 'I must be especially hateful to them as a composer of patriotic music,' he observed at the time. The fighting was conducted with considerable savagery on both sides, and when Järvenpää was taken by Red troops and Ainola was searched 'for arms', Sibelius's friends and relatives prevailed upon him to move into the relative safety of the capital. With a pass signed by the Red commandant, he moved into Helsinki and settled at the Lapinlahti Hospital, where his brother was senior doctor. The Whites with German aid liberated those parts of the country under the Reds, and with the conclusion of hostilities Finland became an independent republic.

CHAPTER IV

1918–1957

FOR Sibelius one consequence of the war was isolation from the mainstream of European music-making. He often bemoaned the fact that he could no longer hear first-class orchestral playing, and he longed for the day when peace would enable him to return to the Continent. The end of the war found him once again immersed in work on the final version of the fifth symphony. This was interrupted by various commissions, an academic march for the university graduation ceremonies of May 1919, a cantata called *Jordens sång* for the inauguration of the Swedish Academy at Turku, and a trip to Denmark for a festival of Nordic music held in Copenhagen in the summer of the same year. Here he conducted his second symphony with conspicuous success. During this period plans were also forming in his mind for two new symphonies.

A tempting offer from America came his way early in 1920; the newly founded Eastman School of Music offered him a chair of composition, which at first he agreed to accept, though he sensibly insisted on an ample salary (20,000 dollars). It was with this contract in his pocket that he made his last visit to England during the winter of 1921, conducting concerts all over the country. He directed the fifth symphony at Queen's Hall at the first of his London concerts and shared the second with his old friend Busoni. Busoni played a Mozart concerto and his own *Indian Fantasy* while Sibelius conducted his fourth symphony. This was the last time they were to meet, for Busoni died three years later. In his memoirs Sir Henry Wood describes the headache their joint visit gave him:

> I could generally manage Busoni when I had him to myself, but my heart was always in my mouth if he met Sibelius. I never knew where they would get to. They would forget the time of the concert at which they were

to appear; they hardly knew the day of the week. One year I was directing the Birmingham Festival and had to commission a friend never to let these two out of his sight. He had quite an exciting time for two or three days following them about from restaurant to restaurant. He told me he never knew what time they went to bed or got up in the morning. They were like a couple of irresponsible schoolboys.[1]

Apart from his travels, which included a concert tour of Norway and Sweden in the early part of 1923, Sibelius still composed prolifically. A vast quantity of miniatures flowed from his pen; the *Valse lyrique*, *Valse chevaleresque*, the *Suite mignonne*, the *Suite champêtre*, and the sets of piano miniatures, Op. 94, 97 and 99, all date from the immediate post-war years. Some of these orchestral pieces were included in the concert he gave on 19th February 1923, when his sixth symphony was presented to the Helsinki public for the first time. Immediately after this he proceeded to Italy, where he conducted his second symphony in Rome, and set to work on his seventh in earnest. The seventh was completed on 2nd March 1924, and was at first known as *Fantasia Sinfonica*. It was under this title that it was first performed in Stockholm three weeks later, but the composer decided in favour of 'Seventh Symphony' by the time the score appeared in print the following year. Performances were not slow in following: Stokowski and Koussevitzky both directed performances in America, though it was not given in Finland until three years after the Swedish *première*.

The following year the Royal Theatre of Copenhagen commissioned incidental music for a lavish production of Shakespeare's *The Tempest*, which was planned for 16th March 1926, and work on this occupied him for more or less the whole of 1925. In December of that year Sibelius celebrated his sixtieth birthday, and tributes, gifts and telegrams were showered on him in even greater profusion than before. The government increased his pension; his Danish publisher Hansen gave him a substantial sum of money; and he received the proceeds of a nation-wide fund launched to pay him tribute and totalling 150,000 Finnish marks. Again no sooner had December passed than

[1] *My Life of Music* (London, 1938), pages 141–2.

SIBELIUS WALKING NEAR HIS HOME

he made his customary pilgrimage to Italy and there worked on two commissions: the first for a choral work of no great importance (*Väinön virsi*), the second from New York, asking for a tone-poem. The outcome of this was *Tapiola*, which first saw the light of day on 26th December 1926 under the baton of Walter Damrosch.

After *Tapiola* Sibelius produced no major work, though he continued to compose. There were many small-scale works published during the latter part of the twenties, such as a march for male chorus, the *Masonic Ritual Music,* Op. 113, and in 1931 funeral music for organ, *Surusoitto*. Later on he revised earlier works, including two of the *Lemminkäinen* legends, and according to Harold Johnson[1] even dictated a new accompaniment for one of his songs from *Twelfth Night* as late as 1957, the year of his death.

Rumours of an eighth symphony were current for many years; it was promised several times during the early thirties. The prospectus of the Sibelius Society, founded in London by H.M.V. in June 1932, announced that it would include the new symphony in the six volumes of records that it planned to issue, while later in the same year the work was promised to Koussevitzky to conclude the cycle of all the Sibelius symphonies which he was giving in Boston that season. It is probable that an eighth symphony did exist in some form or other at this time; rumour had it that Sibelius had even delivered it into the hands of his publisher, but woke him up in the middle of the night to demand its return, while one story runs that the work was even put into rehearsal. The composer told Basil Cameron in 1945 that the work was 'finished' on many occasions, but he had not been satisfied with it. It would seem pretty certain that it was nearing completion in 1932–3 when he made at least two promises to deliver the score, but that he became increasingly dissatisfied with it. No doubt the appearance of Cecil Gray's books during the early thirties and the reverence in which Sibelius was coming to be held in the Anglo-Saxon world at this time made the composer cautious about releasing a score which he did not feel to be a worthy successor to the other seven. Apart from the Sibelius Society, the visits of Kajanus to London in 1930 and 1932,

[1] *Jean Sibelius* (New York, 1959; London, 1960), page 203.

and of the Finnish National Orchestra under Georg Schnéevoigt two years later, had stimulated a growing appetite for Sibelius's music, while in 1935 an inquiry among listeners to the New York Philharmonic Society's broadcasts revealed that he outstripped any other composer in popularity.

Sibelius's life during these last years was uneventful. Despite press rumours that he was accompanying the Finnish Orchestra on their visit to London in 1934, and subsequently that he would attend the six concerts of his music also given there in January 1938, he gave up travelling. He conducted a broadcast of his *Andante festivo* for a short-wave programme beamed to the New York Fair in January 1939, but that again was a special exception to his retirement. In 1939 Europe was again plunged into war, though Finland was not at first involved. In November, however, the Soviet Union, having seized the Baltic states, launched an attack on Finland. Sibelius received more than a hundred offers of refuge abroad, but declined them all; wild rumours circulated, one of them claiming that he had been killed in an air raid. He made a radio appeal for American help on 30th November, and a stamp with his head and the words 'I need your help' was released in America to raise funds for the Finnish cause. The cruel war ground on to its bitter and inevitable end, and the Finns signed the instrument of peace early the following year, ceding the Karelian Isthmus and other territory in the north. With the Nazi attack on Russia in 1941, Finland took the opportunity of retrieving her losses in territory, but instead of stopping at the 1939 frontier foolishly involved herself in a full-scale punitive attack on Russia proper. When the German invaders were thrown back in 1944 and a separate peace was sought, their German allies exacted a bitter and ruthless vengeance on the Finnish populace.

The privations of the war years left their mark on Finland. In early April 1945 *The Times* carried reports that Sibelius was in need, and the question of help was mooted. Though the reports were denied, public reaction both in England and America gave an idea of the firm hold he enjoyed on public affection. Few great composers have received such recognition and inspired such devotion in their own lifetime. On the occasion of his eighty-fifth birthday the President of Finland even motored out to Järvenpää to pay the nation's respects; while on his ninetieth in 1955 he received no fewer than 1,200 telegrams, presents from all the Scandinavian monarchs, specially recorded tapes from Toscanini, cigars from Sir Winston Churchill, and, as usual on his birthday, special arrangements had to be made to cope with the volume of parcels and mail. President Passikivi broadcast a birthday message, special radio programmes were arranged all over Scandinavia, while the ninetieth birthday concert given in London by Sir Thomas Beecham was relayed to Finland on an especially powerful signal so that the composer could hear it at Ainola. Even before this, the conservatoire he had attended had been renamed after him, a Sibelius Museum was set up at Turku (Åbo), an annual Sibelius Festival was instituted, as well as a Sibelius Prize whose recipients included Stravinsky, Shostakovich and Hindemith. More than fifty streets have been named after him (including one in so improbable a place as Jamaica), and there are several parks also bearing his name.

In spite of this Sibelius's last years were for the most part quiet. Constant disturbance by tourists caused him to retire more firmly into his shell. His correspondence had for many years become so voluminous that he had to engage a secretary,[1] but visitors were rarely permitted. The family itself was a large one—five daughters, fifteen grandchildren and twenty-one great-grandchildren—so that even they had to exercise restraint if Sibelius and his wife were to have any peace. The very necessary measures he took in self-protection against troublesome visitors earned him the reputation of aloofness and pride, though all who met him have testified to the contrary. There was a complete absence of haughty reserve; his personality was spontaneous, warm and immediate.

Though Sibelius had not always enjoyed perfect health (indeed at the time of his marriage he was so delicate that Aino was often warned that she would be nursing an invalid for the rest of her life), he was for the most part untroubled by serious physical ailments. and certainly enjoyed a robust constitution. He was well right up to the very end of

[1] Sibelius's secretary, Santeri Levas, is at present engaged in a comprehensive memoir, the first part of which was published in 1957.

his life. Death came on 20th September 1957. He had been normal and active earlier in the day, and read the morning papers as usual. However, after lunch he collapsed with cerebral haemorrhage: he was fully conscious until about four in the afternoon and recognized members of the family who gathered round him. He died during the evening while in Helsinki the orchestra under Sir Malcolm Sargent was playing his fifth symphony. The State funeral took place ten days later in the *Storkyrkan*; the slow movement of the fourth symphony, *In Memoriam* and *The Swan* were among the music played. Wreaths were laid by the President, and Aino and other close relatives, and the funeral oration was given by Kilpinen. He was laid to rest in the grounds of his villa at Järvenpää, where he had lived for more than fifty years.

To form an accurate and well-focused picture of Sibelius the man is not easy. Even some of the more familiar photographs are misleading, for he was not the unsmiling Nordic giant with features of granite that many of these pictures would lead us to believe. To begin with, he was no giant: a photograph taken in 1919 at the Nordic Music Festival in Copenhagen [1] shows him to be distinctly smaller physically than one imagined from some of the formal photographic studies. Here he is in fact much smaller both in stature and build than either Stenhammar or Halvorsen, and not much taller than Nielsen. While this is of no importance whatever, it does serve as an example of the false impression that has gained currency. There is no denying the enormous power of his features, which are often firm-set and forbidding, but Sibelius rarely felt at ease before the photographer's lens and rarely relaxed his guard. He was basically shy and reserved, though once the initial protective barrier had been overcome and he had warmed to a person he was impulsive, generous and unselfconscious. Gordon Bryan, who visited him regularly at Järvenpää, spoke of the complete absence of pretence and 'side', while Cecil Gray in his autobiography [2] tells of his powers as a host:

[1] *See* Harold Johnson, *Jean Sibelius* (New York, 1959), facing page 145.
[2] *Musical Chairs* (London, 1948), pages 256–7.

His English not being good, and my Finnish and Swedish non-existent, we floundered about in a curious macaronic language compounded of French and German. After a few minutes of polite, but very strained, conversation in this idiom, I must have made some observation which pleased him for he suddenly exclaimed: 'But, Mr Gray, you are not a journalist—you are a musician! Why did you not say so at the start?' He became a different man, jumped up, shook hands with me warmly, produced a bottle of whisky from the cupboard, and from that moment onwards all went well. When we parted it was arranged that I should lunch with him the next day at the hotel where he always stayed on his visits to the Finnish capital.

Not only did he prove to be the perfect host in all that pertains to the table, but the intellectual feast he spreads before his guests is even more magnificent. . . . Of himself and his work he speaks diffidently and unwillingly. One quickly realizes that he prefers to discuss any and every subject on earth—literature, philosophy, painting, politics, science. Suddenly, on looking around the restaurant, I noticed that we were the only people present and, glancing at my watch, discovered that it was about six o'clock, Murmuring a few words of apology for having outstayed my welcome, I made as if to depart; but my host appeared mildly surprised at the suggestion, and prevailed upon me to stay for dinner, which we duly consumed at the same table. We did not separate until seven o'clock in the morning.

His love of the pleasures of the table was acquired long before the thirties when Gray saw him. They date back to his youth and the famous 'Symposium' evenings when Sibelius, then in his late twenties, Kajanus, the poet Gallén-Kallela, and one or two friends used to meet for lengthy discussions stimulated by quantities of wine. A portrait of Sibelius looking rather the worse for wear won these evenings some notoriety at the time.

His love of the classics and his insatiable appetite for reading were childhood passions which never left him. The extent and variety of his literary interests are evident from the large and impressive library at Ainola. The poetry of his native Swedish remained an enduring love, but he was more fortunate than many Swedish-speaking Finns of his class in receiving instruction in a Finnish-speaking school, which gave him access to the world of the *Kalevala* in its original form. This work fired his imagination throughout his life. Naturally enough he spoke Swedish better than Finnish, though he was remarkably sensitive to the musical inflexions of the Finnish tongue. With his marriage into a Finnish family he came gradually to correspond in that language, though at first in writing to Aino he wrote in Swedish and she in Finnish. With his children he spoke Swedish for the most part, though later in life he seems to have preferred Finnish.[1] The important thing, however, is that he was completely bilingual, a Finn first and foremost rather than a member of either the Finnish proper or Finno-Swedish community. With foreign visitors he seems to have spoken a mongrel language of his own, drawing on the first word that came to hand from German, French, Italian or English. He was not a good linguist in the sense that he could speak all these tongues fluently, but he certainly read them with reasonable comfort.

Sibelius's interest in contemporary music was well known. He always seemed to find something kindly to say to younger composers in need of encouragement, and his patience in this matter emerges in Bengt de Törne's portrait of him.[2] He followed musical developments on the Continent and in this country with keen interest even when his sympathies were not directly involved. Among his younger contemporaries Bartók greatly excited his admiration and he spoke highly of many English composers of the older generation including Bax, who, like Vaughan Williams, dedicated his fifth symphony to him. He also spoke appreciatively of Britten's *Peter Grimes* and seems to have maintained a healthy curiosity about new developments in music until his last years. The reason for the long 'silence from Järvenpää' will continue to give rise to speculation. The answer may be the simple drying up of the mainsprings of his creative powers, as was the case with Rossini and Glazunov, or it may be a good deal more complex. During the thirties and forties we were told that he was still composing. Mr Basil Cameron is on record as having seen the eighth symphony. Yet at his death it was announced that no major work survived after *Tapiola*. Small wonder at the rumours one still encounters in Finland.

[1] According to Mrs Lauri Kirves, the composer's grand-daughter, Sibelius mostly spoke Finnish with the grandchildren, though in moments of excitement he would revert to Swedish.

[2] Bengt de Törne, *Sibelius—A Close-up* (London, 1937).

It is, of course, difficult to foresee the path he would have taken after *Tapiola*, but it would be no less difficult to imagine the fifth symphony after the fourth or the seventh after the sixth. Sibelius's creative evolution is as mysterious and unpredictable as it is individual. In the absence of concrete evidence it would seem more likely that there was some purely physical decline that affected his creative powers without impairing his outward personality. This is pure speculation, but it makes better sense than the view of the composer ridden with excessive self-doubt. Self-criticism no doubt played its part in the suppression of the eighth symphony, heightened by an awareness of the claims made by Gray, Downes and other critics, but it is not, surely, all the story.

CHAPTER V

THE SYMPHONIES—I

SIBELIUS's earliest compositions were all instrumental, and it was not until the early nineties that he turned to the orchestra. His first orchestral piece was an overture produced during his student days in Vienna, and once launched on the medium he rapidly developed an unfailing ear for idiomatic and individual orchestral sonorities. But with each successive step—the *Kullervo* symphony, *En Saga*, the *Karelia* music and the four *Legends*—came a heightened awareness of colour and a growing mastery of orchestral resource. Even in the *Kullervo* symphony, his first large-scale work, written only a year or so after the overture, we find a vivid orchestral imagination; and only a few years were to pass before the assurance he showed in handling the medium ripened into genius.

But it is not merely the astonishing growth of his orchestral instincts that marks his development during the nineties. Comparison of the first movement of *Kullervo* with that of the first symphony will show what enormous strides Sibelius had made as a symphonic thinker during the seven years that separate the two works. He was thirty-three by the time he came to write the first symphony and spoke as a mature, creative personality with an impressive list of works behind him. While he does not satisfy all the demands made by a symphony, the first movement comes nearer to perfection than any of his other works up to that time with the exception of *The Swan*. It is in fact a *tour de force* of organic symphonic thinking. The thematic material is more carefully tailored for symphonic treatment than the magnificent but essentially lyrical idea which throbs and surges through the corresponding movement of *Kullervo*. It is true that the earlier work shows an amazingly secure handling of a large-scale design,[1] but it appears sprawling if put alongside the masterly economy of the first symphony.

In a first-class analysis Gerald Abraham has shown how organic this music is [2] and has traced the derivation of the opening motive of the second group, which sparkles away icily to the accompaniment of *tremolando* strings and harp, back to the dark, sombre clarinet theme which opens the work:

Ex. 1 (*a*)

Ex. 1 (*b*)

This is only one of the many examples of the underlying unity of the thematic material. It is an organic process of which Sibelius was almost certainly not conscious. Nils-Eric Ringbom [3] relates a far more obvious similarity between two passages in two different movements of the fifth symphony which Sibelius himself declared to be 'pure coincidence'.

In this first movement we find the full-blooded rhetoric of romanticism wedded to a directness of utterance and economy of design that are truly classical. One could cite as an example of this superb craftsmanship the way in which the confident and assertive climax of the first group flows so swiftly and unobtrusively into the second. While in so many Romantic first symphonies the seams and joins in the structure are clearly visible, this transition is astonishingly smooth and accomplished. This first element of the second group (Ex. 1 (*b*)) later becomes the accompaniment to a second and more important motive

[1] The *Kullervo* symphony is more fully discussed in the chapter on Choral Music, page 107.

[2] *Sibelius, a Symposium* (London, 1946), pages 15 ff.

[3] *Sibelius* (Oklahoma, 1954), page 138.

(Ex. 2), so that at the reprise Sibelius is able to telescope it all together. This second element also gives rise to some of the most powerful and compact writing in the development:

Ex. 2

Sibelius's mastery of transition can be seen in the finale, where he moves from one tempo to another with amazing skill. In his illuminating book on the symphonies[1] Simon Parmet points to the skilful transition from the *Allegro* to the *Andante assai* (the introduction of the contrasting theme) at fig. F in the score; both sections share a common pulse. This facility in handling contrasts of tempo acquires an added dimension later on; two contrasting tempi are maintained simultaneously in some of the later music, and seem to struggle for mastery before one or other gains ascendancy. The seventh symphony affords an excellent example of Sibelius's effortless virtuosity in this respect.

It is the slow movement of the first symphony that most eloquently recalls Sibelius's debt to the Russians.[2] Whether or not Sibelius knew the work of Balakirev or Borodin at this time, he must certainly have encountered Tchaikovsky on his numerous visits to the Continent during the nineties. We must remember that the *Pathétique* had been written only six years previously. The lush opening theme of the *Andante* and the big tune of the finale suggest the higher, more feverish, emotional temperature of the Russian composer. The tune in the finale is unmistakably Tchaikovskian, an unafraid demonstration of melodic feeling. The fact remains that none of the other movements can be said to match the first in poetic intensity or organic cohesion. The melodic inspiration, though powerful on occasion, is less individual; the links which bind the part to the whole, the moment

[1] *The Symphonies of Sibelius* (London, 1959), page 6.

[2] There is a striking correspondence between the second group of the first movement of Tchaikovsky's *Souvenirs de Florence* and the figure at bar 84 of Sibelius's slow movement.

to the movement, are less securely forged. The scherzo, it is true, has a compelling physical excitement and some characteristic woodwind writing, and it is perhaps in the finale that the weaknesses become most readily apparent.

The movement begins with the clarinet theme which opened the work, though at a much higher level of intensity, being passionately declaimed by the strings. It also ends with the same two *pizzicato* chords in E minor as did the first; but here the similarity ends. The movement operates on an altogether different level, and the tension which it generates is that of melodrama rather than high tragedy; there is much thrilling orchestral detail, sudden and vivid dramatic contrasts, impetuous and declamatory outbursts of rhetoric, but the excitement is from moment to moment rather than the outcome of a cumulative increase of tension over a longer time-span. Although there is much that is characteristic in the last three movements and many pages of a stark and arresting beauty, the level of inspiration is distinctly inferior to that of the *Legends*.

Sibelius waited only two years before embarking on another essay in this form. The second symphony breathes much the same air as the first, and in this work, too, it is the opening movement which makes the deepest impression. The air of apparent relaxation and effortlessness with which this sunny, genial music unfolds serves to obscure its immense strength; in the same way Sibelius's seemingly casual approach to his thematic ideas misleads the listener as to its intensely organic nature. Many of the ideas seem to belong to each other or derive from a common seed, though when they are more closely scrutinized their relationship becomes more elusive and less easy to define. But each motive evolves naturally from its predecessor, and even when one idea merely echoes another, as it does at the beginning of the symphony, it grows spontaneously and organically out of the texture and takes on an independent life of its own. The horn motive, which punctuates the main woodwind theme, is an instance in point. How skilfully and unobtrusively Sibelius dovetails the first horn entry into the texture! It emerges from the theme not merely as an echo of the cadential figure (marked *x*) but as an idea in its own right:

Ex. 3

The use of a succession of thematic strands rather than long, predictable, obviously connected melodic paragraphs led Cecil Gray in his study of the symphonies to assume that Sibelius was breaking entirely new ground in his treatment of sonata form, whereas in actual fact he does nothing that cannot be explained in terms of traditional sonata procedure. Admittedly, one melodic idea does not appear to dominate either the first or second groups, though one of the elements of the latter does assume a more dominating role in the development. To speak of a second 'subject' in this context is therefore unwise (as it is, in fact, in so many classical works), and to isolate the oboe tune at fig. B, as Parmet does on the grounds that it is 'best suited to serve as the second theme, as it offers a greater contrast to the main theme than any other thematic idea',[1] belies in some measure the genius of

[1] *Op. cit.*, page 17.

this exposition. It is the amazing diversity of character contained in the second group that distinguishes it from the mildness of the pastoral first group. Here is the motive in question:

Ex. 4

While this idea can be said to open the second group, the most important single element is the woodwind figure, in which a downward leap of a fifth is prominent. It will be observed that the accompaniment is that of the opening, though the tone is more emphatic and urgent, and by the end of the movement we are left in no doubt that there is an especially close relationship between the first and second groups in this piece:

Ex. 5

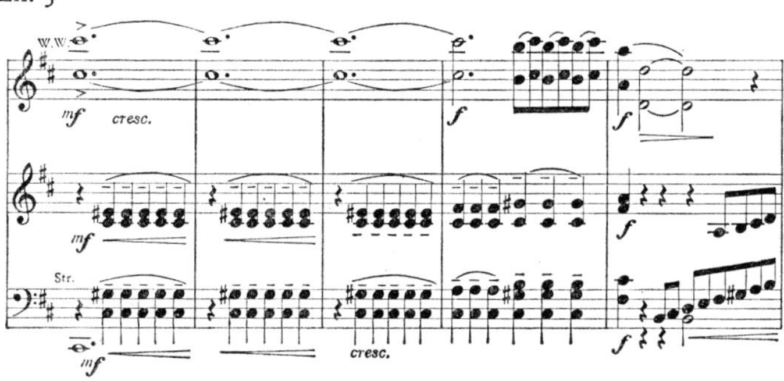

A turbulent motive which springs from this and generates a good deal of excitement returns us to the dominant: the woodwind develop the downward fifth into an angry comment which is of some importance in the development.

The exposition is a fine example of the extraordinary freedom and assurance which Sibelius shows in his approach to sonata form. The fact that several authorities dispute the identity of the second 'subject', while yet another maintains that there is not one at all, speaks for itself; and indeed, to dogmatize about this exposition in purely academic terms, with hard-and-fast divisions between the first group, the transition material and the second group, is impossible. One thing that will strike the student of Sibelius the closer he examines this symphony is the fact that no one fragment, idea or motive in the initial statement is wasted. In spite of the lushness of the idiom in comparison with, say, the third and fourth symphonies, the movement betrays no less a degree of integration and cohesion; and it is certainly more remarkable in that respect than the corresponding movement of the first symphony. There is no surplus flesh on this lithe Attic figure.

Take as an example the very opening of the development. Here the oboe begins with Ex. 5, but from now on this melody is more often than not associated with the bassoon idea which darkly answers it. While the actual contour is new, this bassoon pendant has a close spiritual relationship to the horn motive attached to the first theme. It shares its first three notes and makes an allusion to the rhythm of its cadential figure. The use of the transition material is interesting. At its first appearance in the exposition it seems to bring the first element of rhetoric into the music, an element which is intensified with its impassioned, questioning pendant (marked *x*), from which the second group material so naturally arises:

Ex. 6

The development itself largely tends to concentrate on Exs. 3 and 5, and the material rising out of them; although oblique reference is made to it, the transition material is held in hand until, at the climax, the point of transition from development to restatement, it steers the music back into the tonic in a blaze of triumph. Here the persuasive rhetoric of the violins is exchanged for the massive and eloquent power of the brass.

This point, the opening of the restatement, offers a splendid example of Sibelius's powers of compression. The expressive pendant (Ex. 6, *x*) is used as a counterpoint to the main woodwind theme of the first group: while a few bars earlier Sibelius had reinforced the bond we noticed between the first and second groups by weaving Ex. 4 into the texture and again alloting it the role of a counterpoint to Ex. 3. The remainder of the reprise pursues a fairly normal path, though, as reference to Exs. 4 and 6 has been so recent, they do not return again. It is to Ex. 5, and the material associated with it, that the recapitulation turns.

Again, as with the first symphony, the other movements are by no means as highly concentrated or as perfectly proportioned. Nor, for that matter, do they show the same originality in the handling of the thematic substance, though the ideas themselves are individual enough. But none of these movements reveals so many subtleties on closer analysis as did the first. The second movement, for example, is far more loose-limbed and rhapsodic in feeling than its predecessor, though in layout it falls, roughly speaking, into a species of sonata form. It is of interest to note the modal feeling in much of the material. Modal influences are discernible in the whole of Sibelius's output from *En Saga* and the *Karelia* suite onwards; they were certainly not confined, as Cecil Gray seemed to imagine, to the sixth symphony. Needless to say, this can be largely attributed to the early assimilation of Finnish folk-music into both his melodic style and his harmonic vocabulary. The slow movement is rich in good tunes, and the scherzo which follows it is a brilliant foil with highly effective virtuoso writing for the orchestra. Its trio is also highly characteristic of the composer[1] and reinforces the pastoral undertones that one feels in the first movement.

After this the 'big tune' in the finale seems rather lame, even banal. It is in fact the only movement in all seven symphonies to come near

[1] The famous oboe melody is said to be based on a Czech folk-tune which Sibelius heard while in Prague.

to bombast. It goes through the motions of sonata form, has two widely contrasted themes, and provides a stirring climax to the work; but nevertheless it is not a worthy bedfellow of the first movement, and put alongside it the invention seems thin, the gestures empty. The expansion of the second theme when it recurs in the restatement compels admiration, perhaps by its very tenacity and insistence, though it comes dangerously close to the world of rabble-rousing patriotic music to which Sibelius often lent the odd moment. These less lofty emotions similarly seem to govern the temper of the overblown peroration. This movement does not quite match the demands made by the rest of the work, and musically must be regarded as the weakest single movement in all his symphonies.

SIBELIUS AT THE TIME OF THE FOURTH SYMPHONY

CHAPTER VI

THE SYMPHONIES—2

THOUGH both early symphonies spring from the soil of Romanticism, they offer convincing evidence of Sibelius's classical sympathies. The first movements are, in both cases, remarkable achievements by the highest standards; and even though the fevers of Tchaikovskian romanticism run high in some of the other movements, the musical ideas are erected on firm, solidly designed structural foundations. However, in terms of sheer originality both of conception and execution, of content and form, the early symphonies must yield pride of place to the symphonic poems. No movement in either symphony is as perfect in design and inspiration, or as rich in poetry, as *The Swan* or *Lemminkäinen in Tuonela*, and nowhere in these symphonies does the composer equal, let alone surpass, the taut, sustained, hair-raising symphonic finale of the four *Legends*. With the third symphony, however, work on which occupied him from 1904 to 1907, this perspective began to change. This was the period of *Pohjola's Daughter* and *Nightride and Sunrise*, as well as of the revision of the violin concerto; but it also saw the composer of masterly symphonic poems firmly launched on his conquest of the symphony.

Various claims have been made for the third symphony. It is certainly more classical in feeling and restrained in utterance than either of its predecessors; it is so cogently argued that one is reminded of Ralph Wood's comments: 'It is paradoxical but true that a work by Brahms or Dvořák or Tchaikovsky is a good deal easier to follow than one by Sibelius, not because there is more connectedness in any of the former but because there is less.'[1] Professor Abraham himself has gone even further in discussing the first movement of this symphony: 'In clearness and simplicity of outline, it is comparable with a Haydn or Mozart first movement. . . . Nevertheless, the organic unity of the movement is far in advance of anything in the Viennese classical

[1] In *Sibelius, a Symposium*, edited by Gerald Abraham, page 43.

masters; and even the general architecture is held together in a way that had classical precedents but had never before, I think, been so fully developed.'[1]

Whether or not this is the case, the fact remains that there is no more perfect instance of classical sonata form in all Sibelius than the first movement of this symphony. It is much simpler to analyse than the corresponding movement of the second, but the relationship between the various thematic elements is no less organic, the feeling of their belonging together no less intense; and the sense of inevitability is, if anything, more marked. The natural flow of the music is uninterrupted by moments of rhetoric, its contours are firm, its idiom is purer: the opulent orchestral colouring of the second symphony is abandoned for a more restrained palette, the glowing hues yield to subtler pastel shades. The actual composition of the orchestra in the two symphonies does not differ in essentials; both include double woodwind, four horns, three trombones, timpani and strings. The second symphony, however, calls for three trumpets as against two in the third and further reinforces its brass by the addition of a tuba. It is obvious that it is the approach to the orchestra and its treatment that differ. One thing is immediately striking: throughout the exposition practically all the important melodic material, including the first and second 'subjects', the closing idea of the second group, as well as the bulk of the musical argument, is given to the strings. In actual fact they are at no point silent during the exposition and, indeed, in the whole movement there are only sixteen bars where they are completely inactive. The pregnant opening bars, with their symmetrical, firmly sculptured outline and their measured rhythmic contour, leave the listener in no doubt as to the classical temper of the movement:

Ex. 7

[1] *Op. cit.*, page 22.

As usual in Sibelius, there is no excess flesh on this vital, athletic body of a movement. An apparently insignificant idea (bar 17) generates a flood of semiquavers that sweeps the music onwards and periodically rises to a torrent that carries all before it. Another entry on the horns a few bars later is more than a climactic flourish; both in outline and rhythm it carefully prepares the ground for the second theme:

Ex. 8

Ex. 9

After the statement of the second theme the semiquaver figure returns as a kind of *ostinato*. From this texture the woodwind call up echoes of the second subject; and thus, as in the first movement of the second symphony, elements of both groups are united within the exposition. Either this passage or similar writing in the development 'is said to represent the composer's impression of fog-banks drifting along the English coast'.[1] Both the development and the restatement follow time-honoured, instinctive procedures. There is an undercurrent of melancholy resignation in the coda, a feeling which is more explicitly stated in the second movement. The actual theme of the coda is entirely new, though it seems related to the closing idea of the exposition; but, as is often the case in the symphonies, the relationship is not one of contour (though for the best part of three bars they share the same rhythmic pattern) but a less easily defined kinship of spirit.

The second movement is by contrast one of Sibelius's least complicated symphonic movements. It is a series of gentle ruminations on a supple wisp of a theme, much of whose charm derives from the metric interplay between 6/4 and 3/2. Those who are familiar with Kajanus's remarkable recording of this work made during the thirties will know that this movement runs a good deal deeper than one would imagine on hearing the average concert or broadcast performance. There is a note of gentle sorrow about the music which becomes very intense in the writing for divided cellos (fig. 6),[2] and the lightening of the atmosphere later on at fig. 10 is merely transient. The tonality centres on G sharp minor, a marked contrast to the outer movements, which are both in C.

From the point of view of structure the finale is the most interesting (and certainly the most original) of the three movements. It falls into two quite clearly defined sections, approximately equal in length; in

[1] Tovey, *Essays in Musical Analysis*, vol. ii (London, 1935), page 123. This sort of remark, along with Sibelius's penchant for overtly programmatic symphonic poems, has encouraged some fanciful writers to try to find literary programmes for the symphonies. No task could be more fruitless, for few symphonies are laid on such sound structural foundations or can stand so firmly on their own feet. Sibelius's exchange with Mahler during the latter's visit to Helsinki in 1907 (the year in which this work was composed) bears this out: 'When our conversation touched on the symphony,' Sibelius told Ekman, 'I said that I admired its style and severity of form, and the profound logic that created an inner connection between all the motifs. This was my experience in the course of my creative work. Mahler's opinion was just the opposite. "No!" he said, "The symphony must be like the world. It must be all-embracing."'

[2] Eulenburg edition.

this respect it might be regarded as a forerunner of the first movement of the fifth symphony, though there the two sections are not approximately equal. In the case of the fifth, some writers (among them Parmet and Gray) maintain that the first movement does in fact constitute two separate movements, and they marshal impressive evidence for this. There can, however, be no question of this here. The first part can well be treated as the exposition and development of a straightforward sonata-form movement. The exposition lays out the two main groups, the second being in the relative minor; the two 'subjects' are both terse, pregnant ideas: the first moves stepwise, the second, on the other hand, makes use of triadic leaps and traces a bolder, more incisive outline. Sibelius makes the same material serve for both the second idea and the accompanying string *ostinato* from which it arises. This *ostinato* is trochaic in rhythm and recalls similar writing in *Nightride and Sunrise*, which was completed at about the same time.

Before the development section the music momentarily returns us to C, almost in the manner of a rondo, and the first idea is again heard on the oboes. The fact that the development is dominated by the second theme, and that in its original form the first idea does not recur, may well explain its reappearance at this juncture.

The second part of the movement replaces the normal recapitulation section: it is concerned with a new idea, a theme of great power and eloquence, which gathers energy as it is reiterated in an atmosphere of growing excitement. The closing bars are worth quoting, for it is this segment which seems to drive the music forward relentlessly:

Ex. 10

The theme is at first stated gently by the strings, but later, as the tension mounts, they provide an *ostinato* while the woodwind and horns take up the melody. The theme, as is always the case in Sibelius, seems to have emerged quite naturally and spontaneously from the context of the movement; there does seem at first sight a connection with the horn figure which can be heard at the beginning of the development, but there is no direct rhythmic or melodic affinity. As a glance at Ex. 10 will show, the fourth note of the scale is sharpened, and this, together with a tendency to move within a limited compass, is a feature of the first subject itself. The entire concept of this movement is strikingly unified and original; and the work as a whole is the first of Sibelius's symphonies that is throughout worthy of his genius.

If the third symphony sounds a note of classical understatement, it is the fourth which, by general consent, enshrines the essential Sibelius. In this work he has distilled a language more economical and concentrated than in any other of his works (with the possible exception of *Tapiola*). The melodic language is more rarefied and allusive, the exploitation of tonality more subtle and complex, and the organization of the work is conceived far more as a totality than in the earlier symphonies. We have already observed that in the first two symphonies the mastery evinced in the first movements is not matched in the later movements; and even in the third symphony the middle movement, underrated though it is, is not pitched on quite the same level as the other two. With the fourth symphony, however, Sibelius's planning is far more comprehensive, the symphony being conceived as a whole much in the same way as the seventh: each of the four movements is a member of one living organism.

Sibelius spoke of the fourth symphony as a reaction against 'modern trends', and there seems little doubt that he had in mind the large canvases and opulent colours of Mahler and Strauss. Certainly its restraint in using the full orchestra, the lack of self-indulgence of any kind, and the austerity of its musical language, place it at the opposite pole from Mahler. Its austerity earned it the title of the *Barkbröd* symphony in Scandinavia—a grim reminder of the hard days in the nineteenth century when starvation compelled some of its victims to eat the bark of trees. Although only three years had elapsed since the third symphony (the fourth was begun in 1910 and finished the following spring), the very opening bars emphasize the immense distance Sibelius had travelled in terms of self-discovery. The firm line, regular phrase structure and unambiguous tonality of the first bars of the third symphony contrast markedly with the dark brooding intensity of the fourth. The confident, optimistic temper of No. 3 is laid aside: here the mood is despondent, the rhythm hesitant and the tonality obscure.

The first four notes come to assume considerable importance in the melodic thinking of the first movement: they unobtrusively outline three whole tones, C, D, E, F sharp:

Ex. 11

A minor is soon established, and the cellos and basses settle down to a slow, regular oscillation between E and F sharp, while a solo cello intones the main theme, the first segment of which is triadic in outline. The second group centres on F sharp: first, the brass insinuate themselves into the texture with some savage chords to which there is an impassioned response from violins and violas, in which Ex. 11 is spread-eagled over an additional octave, giving it a certain rhetorical emphasis and a new colouring:

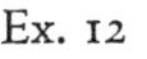
Ex. 12

Secondly, there follows a fleeting motive from the horns, a more tranquil fanfare in the subdominant of the new key; and thirdly, a figure of some majesty on trumpets and trombones. All three themes—or rather motives, for they are so fragmentary in character—firmly establish the new tonal centre, and it is while we are still in F sharp that Sibelius makes further allusion to the first group material. Here the insignificant opening notes are seen to possess an importance that one had not imagined at their appearance. While the main theme is heard in the strings (softened by added thirds), variants of Ex. 11 emerge on the woodwind. All this is a convenient procedure which enables Sibelius to transplant much of this section in the reprise, and thus telescope the initial statement of the first group. When Ex. 11 recurs at the end of the movement it brings with it the severe, cold atmosphere in which the work began, though its key centre has been firmly anchored in the tonic.

The development itself contains some of the strangest music that Sibelius ever wrote. Echoing, perhaps, the tonal uncertainties with which the work began, the melodic line itself assumes an angularity unusual in Sibelius. The contrast in colour at the beginning of the development also serves to enhance the sense of mystery that inspires this music. The warmth of woodwind, horns and lower strings, together with the security of F sharp major, are abandoned for a bleak solo cello [1] and a tonality that is rapidly obscured:

Ex. 13

A little later the strings begin to rustle evocatively, and in the 'whole-tone' texture that ensues we can trace references to Ex. 11, while flutes and clarinets, and later bassoons, cellos and double-basses, give ominous reminders of the tritone. A recurrent timpani pedal point on A serves as a preparation for the foreshortened reprise.

[1] In an article, 'Sibelius fjärde symfoni—en stråkkvartet?', published in the Swedish-language Helsinki paper *Nya Pressen* (7th June 1958), Harold Johnson advanced the theory that much of the material of the fourth symphony was originally intended as a string quartet. There is no doubt that in places Sibelius's scoring in this symphony is extremely chamber-like, and in addition there are few *tuttis*. However, he thought directly in terms of orchestral colour, and it is highly unlikely that any of the work as it stands could have been transplanted from any other medium. If or when the sketches of this work are made available (Johnson did not have access to them), it will be interesting to see whether this theory has any foundation.

This remarkably concentrated movement (a mere 114 bars in length) is matched by a similarly terse scherzo. This even compresses the reprise of the scherzo section (initially some 250 bars in length) into a fleeting reference of six bars. The very opening of the scherzo emphasizes the point that each of the four movements reflects a different aspect of the whole; it is as if one were viewing the same magnificent edifice or vista from totally different vantage points. Here Sibelius begins on exactly the same note (A) as the first movement ended, but this tonic note is seen in a new light, that of F major, a key which had been avoided in the first movement. Over a string *tremolo* the oboe dances in a plaintive, pastoral fashion, avoiding for some time the note B flat; thus the tonality acquires a certain modal flavouring and the interval of a tritone inevitably appears. Later on in the movement the tritone comes to assume great importance, particularly in the menacing trio section, where the main thematic motive persistently hammers this interval against a characteristically Sibelian background of 'transitional harmonies'—a compound of shifting diminished chords, sustained trills that act as pedals in a general atmosphere of harmonic uneasiness where no definite tonality asserts itself.

The third movement may be said to represent the emotional peak of the work. It is contemplative in spirit, and is one of his most profoundly individual and deeply felt utterances. From the opening bars where, against an unsettled tonal background, dark in mood and lonely in feeling, two flutes icily ruminate, to the warm, impassioned climax of the movement, where the main theme is finally and fully set out, there is no superfluous note. The rhapsodic character of the movement emerges at once when the flute soars against a vaguely imitative but highly purposeful bass line. Here we have the most austere yet poetic two-part counterpoint. As Ernest Newman put it: 'The sense of separation from the solid earth that this wide spacing gives us is increased as the flute theme ascends higher and higher and becomes more rhapsodical.' The passage in question is interesting, for it shows that Mahler was not the only composer to think in two widely separated lines bereft of harmonic support. The music makes several attempts to establish C sharp minor and state the lyrical burden of the movement, but the earliest entries of the theme disintegrate, and it is not until we are about half way through that the cellos succeed in stating the theme almost in its entirety, in a C sharp minor context.

Ex. 14

The opening of the finale is in A major, but, as Robert Simpson has pointed out, it presents that key in the light of its relationship with C sharp minor, the key of the preceding movement. Thus the new key has a darker colouring than might have been expected. As in the case of the first two movements, the last two are linked by a pivot-note, the finale opening on the same C sharp with which the *Largo* ended. But the influence of the *Largo* is not confined merely to tonality: there is a direct thematic link between the first theme and Ex. 14:

Ex. 15

This theme has a pendant which echoes the tritone cry that we heard in the first and second movements. This ejaculation is practically all that remains of the first group in the restatement, which is extremely compact. Another development that follows rapidly in the wake of the first group brings home the important dramatic role played by tonality in this symphony. After a longish stretch of 'cross-hatching' on the strings (in A major), the tonic is brought into direct apposition to its furthermost pole (E flat), when a woodwind cry of a third is superimposed on the texture (Ex. 16*a*). This episode closes with a falling seventh (Ex. 16*b*), and these two elements form the basic ingredients of the tragic coda which ends the work:

Ex. 16

It is interesting to note that at the restatement this tonal polarity is preserved, though the roles are reversed; this time the string *ostinato* is in E flat, a somewhat austere precursor of the finale of the fifth symphony, while it is the woodwind that insist on A. The woodwind in fact triumph and bring the music to a conflict involving considerable harmonic tension; this is only right and proper if one recalls that it is the tritone, the *diabolus in musica*, that is being resolved. This conflict has been avoided in the development (or at least postponed), since the music has largely concerned itself with the haunting second group, which rarely settles in one key for any length of time (though at its initial appearance it makes a hasty excursion into E flat). However, the whole of this section and the development move on tonal quicksands and the basic conflict is not brought to issue until the restatement. The coda contains some of the most desolate pages in all Sibelius. The material we have heard in Ex. 16 forms the basis of the musical substance, though the atmosphere is transformed. There is a searching intensity here, a purity of utterance, and a vision and insight of rare quality.

CHAPTER VII

THE SYMPHONIES—3

THE fifth is undoubtedly the most popular of the later symphonies. In comparison with the fourth, with its spare orchestral texture, its colours are opulent and vivid, its mood is heroic, and its idiom easily accessible. The work, in particular its outer movements, is, however, no less fascinating to the student of Sibelius. It seems indeed to have given the composer far more trouble than any of his other symphonies, for after the first performance in 1915 it was withdrawn for revision; a second version, performed the following year, still left the composer unsatisfied, and it was not until 1919 that the work appeared in its final form. The full extent of the alterations that Sibelius made will not be known until the orchestral parts of the first version, which still survive at Ainola, are made available for study. In its original form the work consisted of four separate movements; in the 1916 version the first two movements were played without a break, while, as we know, the final version is cast in three movements.

The first movement has given rise to considerable controversy: a number of writers, including Gray and Parmet, maintain the division into two movements and cite the change of lettering in the score in support of this. There is no doubt that this lettering is a survival from the first cast of the work: the score is marked quite normally until letter N is reached, when, instead of continuing until the end of the alphabet, the lettering begins with A once again. The Finnish musicologist, Erik Furuhjelm, has also observed:

> At the first performances a very short break was made between the two movements or 'parts' in question. This break was indicated in the score. Later, at a meeting with Sibelius (some time during 1916 as far as I remember), the question of this break came up, and during the course of conversation I received the impression that Sibelius considered it to be to the advantage of the work to join the two movements together organically. How soon this

idea was realized I do not know, but it is probable that the alteration was made when the second version of the work was performed at the end of the same year.

The fact that the movements were separate in the first version of the symphony seems to prove, however, that the composer thought of them as I and II in the order of movements, and explains why the rehearsal lettering rather surprisingly begins with A exactly at the point where the second part begins.

Nevertheless, despite this evidence, there are compelling musical reasons for disregarding this division and viewing the piece as one continuous movement. Not the least compelling are the organic cohesion of the material and the overall tonal scheme of the movement.

Most writers are agreed on the first unusual feature of the movement, the double exposition. There are four main thematic strands in the exposition, the first of which is probably the most important:

Ex. 17

The second, which develops quite naturally from the first, is a typically Sibelian woodwind motive in thirds, a discursive figure that prepares the ground for a change of tonality. Throughout the whole of the first group the strings are silent, which lends their intervention in the musical argument additional dramatic force. As it is, they plunge the music into G, the key of the second group, where yet again the woodwind ring out a powerful challenge:

Ex. 18

The fourth element, more agitated and restless in mood, drives home the new key with some degree of urgency. The tonal scheme of the 'counter-exposition' is far less settled. The first reference to the main theme (on the dominant of G) soon leads us through an area of some tonal uncertainty to the tonic; and it is in an affirmation of E flat that the whole exposition ends.

As in most organic processes, it is not always possible to say with any degree of dogmatism where one 'section' ends or another begins (nor, indeed, is there any real reason why one should want to). However, the transition from exposition to development poses no such difficulty, for the opening figure of the development emerges on the horns as the fourth theme gently subsides. This figure, which dominates the music for some time, is in fact the chromatic motive which anticipated the entry of the strings at the first appearance of the second group, though, characteristically enough, it was omitted in the counter-exposition. The writing that follows is among the most starkly original and imaginative in the whole symphony; the ever-shifting currents of the string harmonies, in some ways prophetic of *Tapiola*, provide a background for a long development of this chromatic motive, until the climax at letter L where the second subject (Ex. 18) is heard in full.

A return of the first group in B major leads to the *Allegro moderato* (3/4), the much-discussed second half. Parmet calls this a toccata, while Gerald Abraham offers a more ingenious solution in suggesting that the first hundred bars constitute a scherzo, the next eighty a trio, while the rest can be equated with a scherzo-repeat and recapitulation. While not denying the scherzo-like character of many episodes in the second half of the movement, there is no doubt that it does in fact correspond in broad outline to the recapitulation normal in sonata form. The tonic is re-established at fig. B and material derived from the first subject is brought under review; a new theme, closely related to the first group, is heard on the trumpet:

Ex. 19

There is a good deal of animated, quasi-fugal discussion of this which digresses tonally. However, we soon return to the tonic, where the second subject is heard in a new and magical transformation. Another lengthy and exciting episode of considerable complexity follows before the fourth theme is restated, again in the tonic, and a brilliant coda brings the movement to an end. This movement is one of Sibelius's most original creations, and cannot really be described in terms of the conventional academic moulds; it rests on the foundations of its own inner logic and shows the fallacy of confusing 'form' with long-established, easily recognized musical procedures.

In comparison with this the *Andante* is a simple movement, though it offers ample evidence of the subtlety of Sibelius's thinking. It takes the form of a theme followed by a set of variations; among other things it is a model of the resource and skill with which Sibelius exploits pedal points. The movement is anchored in G major, the key of the second group of the first movement, but the undertone of turbulence and unrest there contrasts with the relaxed and sunny atmosphere that infuses this movement. Twice during the course of the movement Sibelius hints at ideas that are to come in the finale: the basses unobtrusively state the second theme of the finale (five bars after fig. F) and, as Ringbom has pointed out,[1] there are striking similarities between pages 83–4 in the slow movement and 99–100 in the finale.

None of Sibelius's finales offers so large a measure of sheer physical excitement as does the last movement of No. 5. None of the early symphonies can equal its sustained flow of energy; in fact, it is only approached in this respect by the last movement of the third symphony. Sibelius's approach to the problem of the finale is never the same, and although, as in the third, he does make extensive and masterly use of *ostinati* and pedal points, it is the musical content that dictates the direction in which the music is to develop. As in so many of his movements, he moves with complete freedom and does not allow his imagination to be bound by any preconceived academic mould. Parmet calls it 'a kind of rondo', and gives its outline as main theme

[1] *Op. cit.,* page 139 n. (Swedish edition).

—second subject—a short working-out section—main theme—second subject—coda. Conversely, Abraham speaks of it as 'following the outline (though not the key-plan) of sonata form'. In actual fact the use of tonality is highly individual and effective in this movement. There are two main themes, the second of which opens with the famous horn theme which Tovey compared to Thor swinging his hammer.

Sibelius delays his change of key until the very last moment, so that the bulk of the exposition including the second group is in the tonic. The change to C is all the more effective, even though it is not long before the key changes yet again. The reprise begins in G flat with the subdued, mysterious whisperings of the first subject on muted strings. The second also follows in G flat before turning into the tonic minor, where it assumes a grave, melancholy splendour. The final return to the tonic is again heightened by being so delayed, and the awe-inspiring second theme brings the massive, glowing climax and the six famous hammer-blows that end the piece.

If the popularity of the fifth is not hard to explain, neither is the comparative neglect of its successor, for the sixth inhabits a world which is as far removed from the fifth as that, in its turn, is from the fourth. Like the fourth, the sixth symphony has eloquent advocates. The days when one could say that it fell 'between the stools of the appreciation of the many and the appreciation of the few' have fortunately passed, at least as far as the few are concerned. David Cherniavsky speaks of it as 'the final stage in [Sibelius's] quest for, or in his spontaneous attainment of, complete unity', while Ralph Wood calls it 'a dazzling display of a technique so personal and so assured that its very achievements [are] hidden in its mastery and in its entire synthesis with its subject matter'. Neither claim is in the least exaggerated. Nevertheless the sixth does not hold as firm a place in the affections of the general public as either the fifth or the seventh, for it lacks the heroic countenance of the one and the stern epic majesty of the other.

In spite of the addition of a harp to the normal Sibelian orchestra of double woodwind, four horns, three trumpets and trombones, timpani and strings, the scoring is more restrained than in any other

Sibelius symphony. As in the third, it is the strings that carry the main burden of the musical argument. The absence of virtuoso orchestral writing and the physical excitement of massive climaxes do not make for immediate popular appeal, and the refined modal flavouring of the work doubtless seems monotonous to the casual listener. It is clear that Sibelius was highly conscious of the enormous distance between this symphony and the glittering orchestral sonorities of Ravel and Strauss. While they were showing an ever-increasing preoccupation with subtleties of texture and refinements of the orchestral palette, he was working towards homogeneity of form and a greater purity of musical speech. Indeed, it was the feeling of being out of step with the values of his time that prompted his oft-quoted remark, apropos this very symphony, that, while other composers were concocting cocktails of various hues, he offered pure cold water.

In the thirties Cecil Gray hastened to connect the lofty suspensions and profoundly eloquent polyphony of the opening with Sibelius's known admiration for Palestrina, Lassus and the sixteenth-century English masters. He also maintained that its modal atmosphere was unusual in Sibelius's music. In actual fact Sibelius's melodic style bore traces of modal flavouring practically throughout his creative life. What makes the modality of the sixth symphony particularly striking is the greater degree of polyphonic interest at the opening and the greater frequency and impact of modal progressions and cadences.

The kind of symphonic thinking that we encounter in all the late symphonies, and particularly in the sixth and seventh, eludes the conventional analysis of the schoolroom. This music is essentially non-episodic, and is so highly integrated that the outward course it takes does not illuminate the vital organic processes that compel it on its path. But even a study such as that made by Parmet, who shows how the material of the symphony grows from what he calls the *kärnmotiv* or germinal cell, cannot illuminate this process in more than a limited sense. It is a process that is not fully capable of demonstration by any method of verbal analysis. The sense of growth we feel in these symphonies takes place on more than one plane, and the growth and metamorphosis of themes is only one part of the process, though a highly important one. Some of the kinship one feels between two or more ideas cannot be explained solely in terms of similarity (indeed two completely contrasted ideas with no contours or rhythm in common often seem to belong to each other), and to relate each to an initial germinal cell to be found in the work itself, or in the sketches that precede it, or in the imagination of the analyst, is to do so on only one level. This kinship of themes and the feeling of organic cohesion is intimately related to other factors, including the overall tonal design of the work, and cannot be divorced from the constantly changing harmonic and rhythmic context.

In a sense the first movement follows the basic principles of sonata procedure, but it is characteristic of Sibelius's originality that, while agreeing on this basic formal outline, no two writers arrive at identical results. Parmet[1] implies that this is the first subject:

Ex. 20

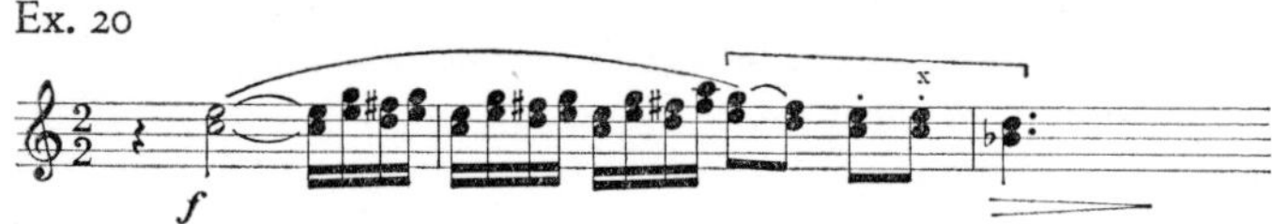

and goes on to say that 'the exposition shows a remarkable irregularity in that the second subject, or something that might be regarded as equivalent, is missing'. He argues, too, that the *Allegro* proper, beginning at fig. B, is the section in which sonata form is used. Abraham,[2] on the other hand, calls this the first (and implies that it is the most important) element of the second group.

Certainly, since it begins an *Allegro*, the theme has the 'feel' of a first subject. Yet in the recapitulation it is the main Dorian tune that returns us to the tonic and assumes the role of first subject, while Ex. 20 does not appear again. In its stead there is a new theme:

Ex. 21

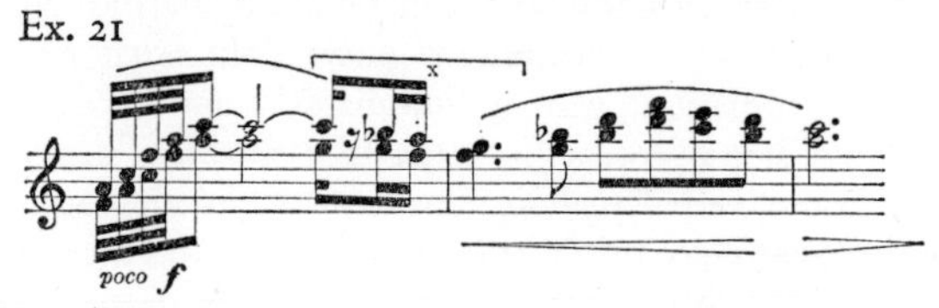

[1] *Op. cit.*, pages 100–1.

[2] *Op. cit.*, pages 32–3.

However, both these ideas have one thing in common, the descending figure *x*, Parmet's *kärnmotiv* from the very opening:

Ex. 22

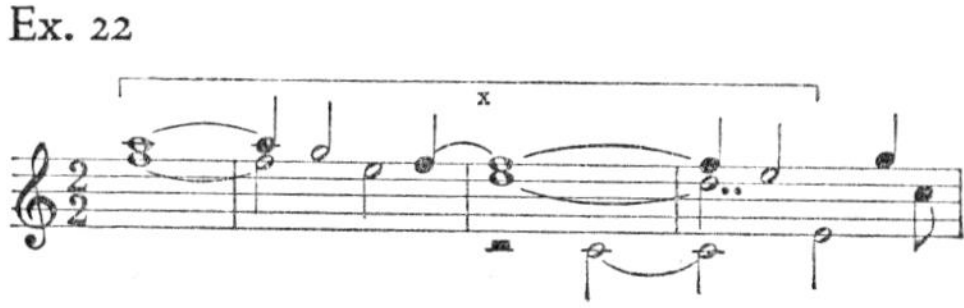

This figure, as we can see, plays an enormous role in the growth of the symphony right until the impassioned outcry on the strings at the very end of the work:

Ex. 23

All this shows the futility of applying labels to the thematic strands in the late symphonies, for the role played by any one of them cannot be strictly defined in academic terms. Sibelius's mastery enables him to move with a freedom so complete that the musical events are dictated by their own inner necessity. They are not governed by any scheme or design imposed from without: that is why no two Sibelius symphonies are alike.

The slow movement (if it can properly be called a slow movement) could not be more characteristic of the composer both in its harmonic inflections and in its elliptical melodic line. The latter is far removed from the melodic style of Tchaikovsky to which Parmet compares it. Its scoring is wonderfully economical. The scherzo, too, is a *tour de force*: the pulse never seems to slacken. The menacing brass chords are used with a power similar to, but different in effect from, those in the fourth symphony. The finale, one of Sibelius's most perfect, opens with an introduction directly related to the opening *kärnmotiv*, just as the main *Allegro* idea takes the main theme of the first movement as its point of departure.

Sibelius planned the sixth and seventh symphonies at much the same time. This element from the first movement of No. 6 (Ex. 24 (*a*)), which plays a part analogous to a second group theme in both the exposition and restatement, is obviously hewn from much the same substance[1] as this lithe, sinewy figure (Ex. 24 (*b*)) from No. 7:

For some writers, among them Ralph Wood, the material of the seventh symphony seems less worthy of Sibelius: indeed in comparing the two Wood has gone so far as to describe it as 'a heroic failure'. The seventh symphony does, however, scale heights quite different from its predecessor, though in purity of utterance and harmony of spirit it does not match the sixth.

There is no reason why it should. Despite its intense concentration of matter, it is epic in character: its triumph is that of the human spirit struggling against immense odds on its quest of exploration. It is difficult, I think, to share Ralph Wood's verdict: 'After not only the beauty but the unsurpassable mellowness and fluency of the sixth symphony, Sibelius completed the heroic failure, a failure which the very indifference of some of the material proves to be the failure of a primarily technical feat, that 1924's seventh symphony is.'[2] The very history of the work makes it clear that it is no conscious exercise in

[1] In an illuminating article, 'Some Aspects of Form in the Symphonies of Sibelius' (*Music Review*, 1949), W. G. Hill points out a large number of thematic correspondences between the various symphonies.

[2] Abraham, *op. cit.*, page 89.

symphonic integration: Sibelius did not set out to write a one-movement symphony. It so happened that he did so almost without knowing it. At the first performance the work was billed as 'Symphonic Fantasia'. Only after this did Sibelius number it among the symphonies. Nor can one readily agree that the thematic material of the work is indifferent.

As it stands, the seventh symphony is an example of symphonic metamorphosis so far-reaching and subtle that it would be impossible to do justice to it without countless music examples. In the first and second symphonies Sibelius had shown the extent of his mastery of normal symphonic practice, and even as early as the first movement of the second we find evidence of a new, searching approach to form. From the third symphony onwards we never find him approaching the symphonic problem in precisely the same way, though there is, at the same time, no conscious formal experimentation: the material of each symphony dictates the course the music is to take. As Ernest Newman has said of *Tapiola*: 'The form is just the logical correlative of the ideas (or rather of the one idea that runs through it all). It is a form that relates only to that idea: it would be inapplicable to any other, and no "professor of composition" could deduce from it any "rules" that could be bottled and given to the student for home application.' With the seventh symphony we find that Sibelius had abandoned all the stereotyped formal conventions of keys, 'subjects', and so on, to achieve unity on his own terms, the form being 'the correlative of the ideas, and therefore, in the final result, not "a form" at all, but simply *form*, a way of setting about things and getting to the desired end that would hold good only of the particular ideas of the particular work'.

There is then no question of a preconceived mould into which musical material is poured, 'no first and second, no egg and no chicken, in the matter of the idea and the form: each just *is* the other'.[1] Although the symphony is in one movement and consists of a continuous and expanding flow of ideas, the character and tempo of the music undergo many changes. These often seem to suggest the

[1] Newman, *Notes for the Sibelius Society* (H.M.V., 1932).

characteristics we normally associate with the conventional symphony; there are times when the music assumes the aspect of a scherzo and others where it seems like a sustained slow movement. The formal layout has been variously described: exposition, development, scherzo and so on, although there is general agreement that these are inadequate 'working labels' and that the symphony is a single indivisible organism. Formal analysis can however be of some help in recognizing some of the more obvious landmarks in the work when the terrain is still relatively unfamiliar. One obvious feature of the landscape is the appearance on three occasions of this theme:

Ex. 25

These appearances form the backbone of the symphony and enshrine its epic character. It has on all three occasions to superimpose itself on a texture of great complexity, and on each appearance the climax is stormier than the previous one. The theme, too, is an important reference point tonally. It always appears in C; in this sense alone, as in many other aspects of its tonal layout, the symphony is comparable to no other.

The process of metamorphosis is set in motion from the very opening bars, a rising scale on the strings. Out of this we come to an important idea which is almost immediately reduced to its skeleton form (*x*) after the repetition of the theme itself:

Ex. 26

Characteristically, too, the very opening and the second theme (Ex. 26, *x*) are telescoped (seven bars after fig. E). One of the most individual fingerprints of Sibelius's craftsmanship is the use of apparently insignificant segments that serve to link more important thematic elements, as vital life-giving motives on their own account later on. The little chromatic figure that links the first and second group in the first movement of the fifth symphony is a good case in point, for it assumes importance in the development. This turn (at fig. A):

Ex. 27 (*a*)

is a case in point for it gives rise to this:

Ex. 27 (*b*)

Who would suspect that the four descending notes that immediately follow would play such an important role in the heroic closing pages?

Ex. 28

Yet this gradually becomes the impassioned figure we encounter at fig. Z. Only a few bars after its first appearance it assumes a gentle, almost resigned, questioning air:

Ex. 29 (*a*)

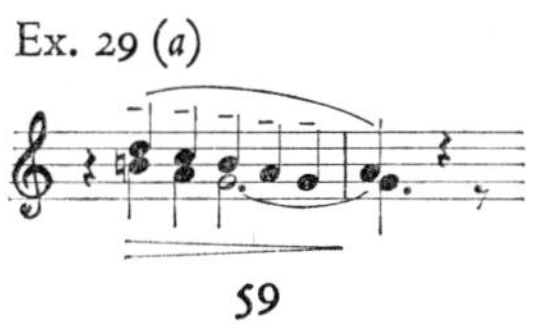

At fig. E we recognize the physiognomy familiar in the great final climax:

The sustained string passage which follows Ex. 28 is one of the most remarkable examples of unbroken polyphony in twentieth-century music. From this idea the motive quoted in Ex. 24 (*b*) is obviously derived. It is in this section too that Ex. 27 makes its impact felt:

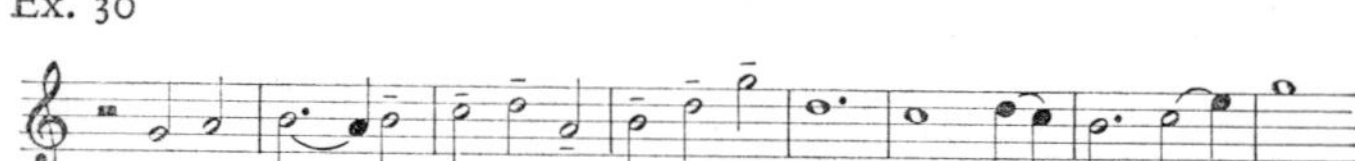

The way in which such themes are constantly renewing themselves is a never-failing source of wonder to the student of this symphony. No subsequent idea, however fresh it may seem, is unrelated to what has gone before. Whether or not Sibelius designed the seventh symphony as a symphony or as a 'fantasia sinfonica', the fact remains that he hardly ever composed a piece more completely original in form, so subtle in its handling of tempo, individual in its handling of tonality, or so wholly integrated in its thematic material. But it is not merely these virtues but the humanism that inspires this music that leaves the listener in no doubt that this symphony is a heroic work, life-enhancing and affirmative in spirit.

CHAPTER VIII

THE SYMPHONIC POEMS

THE symphonic poems are undoubtedly Sibelius's most important works apart from the symphonies. They span practically the whole of his creative career: the first, *En Saga*, was written in 1892 hot on the heels of the *Kullervo* symphony, while *Tapiola*, the last and greatest of them, dates from 1925. Were no other works to survive from his pen, we should still be able to form a fairly comprehensive picture of his development, for most facets of his highly idiosyncratic style are reflected in them. The full-blooded romanticism of his early works appears in *En Saga* and the first of the four *Legends*; the more intimate, introspective aspect of his personality is revealed in *The Bard*; while the full extent of his mastery emerges in *Luonnotar*, *The Oceanides* and the monumental *Tapiola*. Even that aspect of his work which served more to gain popular favour and establish a worldwide reputation than it did to enhance his musical stature is represented by *Finlandia*.

Probably the most important function of the symphonic poem was to serve as a vehicle for Sibelius's interest in Finnish mythology. The symphonic poem had throughout the nineteenth century acted as a convenient outlet for composers discovering their national folklore. Their numbers, particularly in the Slav countries, were legion. But Scandinavian musical nationalism, on the other hand, was slow to develop. Both Gade and Berwald were far more conscious of their links with the classical tradition than they were of their national heritage. It was Grieg who first set Scandinavian nationalism on its feet after the first tentative steps taken by his countrymen, Kjerulf and Nordraak. But they were all miniaturists; Sibelius was the first, working in the larger forms, to show a profound and lasting interest in the folklore as opposed to the folk-music of his native country. The

Kalevala exercised a fascination over him throughout his life, and this found its most natural (though not its only) outlet in the symphonic poem.

The symphonic poem, too, commended itself for purely musical reasons. Sibelius possessed in the most highly developed form the essential prerequisite of a great symphonist—the ability to conceive music organically. In all seven symphonies the long sustained paragraphs grow naturally one from the other, the main thematic elements are subjected to a subtle process of transformation, and the whole is informed by a sense of unity and a feeling of inevitability. It is not surprising that Sibelius's are the most 'symphonic' poems in the literature of music. In them he mobilizes all the artistic discipline of the symphonies along with a much greater freedom of poetic fancy. The matching of musical and extra-musical considerations is a delicate matter, and the one can easily overbalance in favour of the other. It is a tribute to Sibelius's mastery that programmatic considerations never outweigh musical ones. Moreover, such is the soundness of the musical edifice that our appreciation of the music is entirely independent of our knowledge of its programmatic aims.

The dividing line between symphony and symphonic poem had become blurred during the course of the nineteenth century; indeed, many symphonies of the period were little more than inflated tone-poems. With Sibelius the dividing line is clearly defined. However subtle the process of metamorphosis to which the thematic material is subjected, and however masterly the design, the symphonic poems do not match the weight of the symphonies in either content or form. The difference between the two is most clearly discernible in the range and variety of thematic substance. The symphonic poems, mostly intent on evoking some extra-musical image or mood and less ambitious in their purely musical organization, offer less diversity of melodic interest. This is particularly marked in *Tapiola*, which is virtually monothematic.

En Saga, on the other hand, is rich in melodic variety, although its themes are very different from the pregnant ideas encountered in the symphonies. As in the later symphonic poems, the work follows no direct programme but merely evokes something of the atmosphere of a Nordic saga. It originated in an octet for flute, clarinet and strings on which Sibelius had been working during his year in Vienna (1890–1). After its performance in 1893 he withdrew the work for revision, and it is in this revised form that we know it.

The thematic variety we meet in *En Saga* is matched by considerable tonal freedom. The work opens in A minor and ends in E flat minor, its furthermost pole, while the most important key area of the work is C minor and its relative major, E flat. Apart from the coda which, like the introduction, is dominated by the first theme, there are two sections of relative tonal stability. In the first of these the remaining three themes make their first appearance (the last two being in E flat and C minor respectively). In the second the last two themes are restated, this time both in C minor, where after a short interlude of great poetry, an exciting *ostinato* heralds the re-entry of the first theme. It is characteristic of Sibelius's economy of means that the *ostinato* should be a subsidiary idea, which had already appeared as a foil to the fourth theme at its first appearance. This kind of creative thinking is typical of the symphonic writer. In the intervening period the music modulates with great freedom, touching keys as remote as E major, F sharp minor and G sharp minor.

In its original form, however, *En Saga* showed even more freedom of modulation.[1] Here is one example of the way in which the music plunged abruptly into a foreign key:

Ex. 31

[1] *See* Nils-Eric Ringbom's study, *De två versionerna av Sibelius' Tondikt 'En Saga'* (Åbo, 1956), in which he compares the two scores.

When he came to revise the work Sibelius reduced the number and frequency of these modulations. He made the design of the work more taut and compact, reducing it from 952 to 810 bars. The intervening years had brought him much greater assurance and a very real mastery of the most complex problems of musical craftsmanship. Each transition is negotiated with consummate artistry and the seams that one encounters in the earlier version are no longer visible. The duration of pedal points is, strangely enough, much longer in the revised than in the original version; Sibelius was now confident that he could risk a greater simplicity of tonal structure than he felt able to ten years earlier.

In a sense the design of *En Saga* is analogous to sonata form in that there are clearly defined sections corresponding to exposition, development and reprise, but, as always in Sibelius, it is dangerous to append labels to the music. Sibelius possessed a sense of form so highly developed that it was always he who was the master. He never allowed the conventions of classical procedure to initimidate him: each work developed according to the nature and needs of the material with which he was working. None of the themes plays out the role that sonata form would impose on them; yet they are remarkably, indeed symphonically, integrated and seem to possess a close relationship with each other in spite of their differing character. Each is carefully prepared: the second, for instance, is introduced at its first appearance (bar 96, fifteen bars after fig. C) and accompanied by the first, while the third theme (bar 150, fig. F) embodies a nostalgic reference to the second. Evidence of Sibelius's contrapuntal ingenuity is very striking in the following example from the development, where we see how skilfully he combines various elements from his main themes:

Ex. 32

Sibelius's extraordinary feeling for the strings emerges at the beginning of the work. The opening bars are identical in both versions, though the magical (and highly original) effect he secures at bar 30 (five bars after fig. A) with his muted *divisi* strings is a product of the revision and his rapidly growing orchestral imagination. During the middle section we encounter similarly exciting effects, where all the strings play *tremolando* and *sul ponticello*. Even at this early age, as we see too in *The Swan of Tuonela* and *Lemminkäinen in Tuonela*, Sibelius showed an inborn genius for the orchestra; his imaginative and resourceful use of the strings is no doubt closely connected with his own not inconsiderable prowess as a violinist. But even his writing for other instruments is remarkable in its understanding of the potentialities of each. Here is no question of a young composer writing in terms of the keyboard and then translating his score into the medium of the orchestra. Like Berlioz before him, Sibelius thought directly and idiomatically in terms of orchestral colour.

As in Rimsky-Korsakov's *Skazka*, *En Saga* leaves the listener free to supply the programmatic content from his own fantasy. This is not the case with the four *Legends* for orchestra, Op. 22. All these pieces follow the stories from the *Kalevala* which they are supposed to illustrate. The first of them to be written was *The Swan of Tuonela,* which was completed in 1893, the year after *En Saga,* though it was revised two years later. It was originally planned to form the prelude to an opera on which Sibelius was then working, but which he never completed, called *The Building of the Boat.* If the *Kullervo* symphony, the first version of *En Saga* and the *Karelia* music had shown commanding powers of musicianship, *The Swan* is the first sign of absolute genius. It evokes with icy intensity the lines inscribed on the score: these refer to Runo XIV of the *Kalevala,* where Lemminkäinen makes his attempt to shoot the Swan with his crossbow:

> Tuonela, the land of death, the hell of Finnish mythology, is surrounded by a large river with black waters and a rapid current, on which the Swan of Tuonela floats majestically, singing.

The piece is a moving and expressive rhapsody dominated by the haunting timbre of the cor anglais, whose melody floats on an arctic sheen of strings. Beginning in A minor, the cor anglais line wanders widely, drifting from one tonality to another, often quite remote, before the music settles once again in the tonic. The writing for divided strings produces sonorities that are highly individual; even the opening A minor chords have no counterpart elsewhere. The slow and insistent harp *ostinato* in the closing section is one of the many touches of imaginative vision with which this score abounds. It underlines the brooding, evil beauty of this piece of tone-painting.

Its closing section, like many passages in *En Saga,* makes highly effective use of a sustained pedal-point, but nowhere is this practice more extensive than in the first of the *Legends, Lemminkäinen and the Maidens of Saari,* which was written in 1895 and revised two years later. This and its companion piece, *Lemminkäinen in Tuonela,* were withheld after the first performance; they were both revised in 1939 and published by Breitkopf & Härtel as late as 1954. In spite of the staggering beauty of the opening, *Lemminkäinen and the Maidens* is not as highly personal as *The Swan* or *Lemminkäinen in Tuonela.* The economy of means and feeling for proportion are not as marked as in the other three *Legends*. The thematic ideas fall into two categories, the one passionate and tender, and the other rhythmic and dance-like. The story comes from Runo XXIX of the *Kalevala*: Lemminkäinen is the typical hero of Nordic mythology, tough and fearless with more than a touch of Don Juan about him, and this episode tells of his quest for Kyllikki, how he finds her in the country of the Saari, and how she appears indifferent to his love. He remains with the Saari until, taking the first opportunity that presents itself, he elopes with his beloved and proceeds by sleigh to his home.

The two groups of themes alternate: the first represent Lemminkäinen's love for Kyllikki and the second the dancing and other festivities on the island. Though neither *En Saga* nor *The Swan* reveals any trace of Russian influence, this work does. The first group includes a theme distinctly reminiscent of Balakirev's first symphony, full of tenderness and warmth. Other ideas, too, confirm the feeling that Sibelius is succumbing to the spell of the Russian nationalists:

Ex. 33

After the magical introduction (nothing could be more characteristic than these bars), the tonality gravitates towards E flat, where the second group of themes appears. There are three elements (the first at bar 44, the second at 63 and the third at 74), all of which have an important part to play in the proceedings. The tonality is anchored, often for long periods at a time in E flat, by the liberal use of pedal points. But there are some dramatic key changes. There is a daring and effective modulation in the following quotation (bars 197–206), when we see how by means of a pivot note, enharmonically altered (C flat/B natural), Sibelius moves into a distant tonality with great ease:

Ex. 34

There is a good example of Sibelius's economy of means in the coda, where, as the music dies away, fragments of the second group are heard; one of the repeated woodwind cries is itself a fleeting reference to the main theme of this group. As in so many other Sibelius scores, a fragmentary idea that sounds so new and fresh is found to tie up with motives that have occurred earlier. Sibelius's was a mind that had the capacity, developed to a remarkable degree, of constantly illuminating the same basic material. For all its unabashed romanticism, *Lemminkäinen and the Maidens of Saari* shows a careful integration of the melodic ideas, and although it is defective in proportions (the piece is overlong), there is a great deal of fine music in this score.

Its companion piece, *Lemminkäinen in Tuonela*, which was written and revised at the same time, is on a much higher level of inspiration. Its proportions are more finely judged and its material is more compelling and more thoroughly characteristic. The story again follows the *Kalevala* and tells how, in Runo XIV, one of the herdsmen from Pohjola kills Lemminkäinen as he is himself on the point of shooting the Black Swan. The dark waters of the River of Death bear Lemminkäinen's body to Tuonela. The opening bars set this mood with real poetic vision: *tremolando* strings insistently surge forward and convey an awe-inspiring image of the waters that are to bear the hero's body to Tuonela. Superimposed on this at bar 37 is a woodwind cry, a motive which never moves very far away from its initial note, and when it does, returns to it as if drawn by an irresistible magnetic force. The work, roughly speaking, falls into three parts, the outer two being largely concerned with this opening material. There are some immensely impressive and powerful brass suspensions which sear through the texture. The middle section is one of the most inspired passages in all early Sibelius, and it seems strange that the composer should have withheld music of this order for so long. We are plunged abruptly from F sharp minor into A minor with magical effect. The transition is beautifully contrived: the final element of the main motive (marked *a*) is transformed by the clarinet before being passed to the strings, who intone it with gentle, icy insistence:

Ex. 35

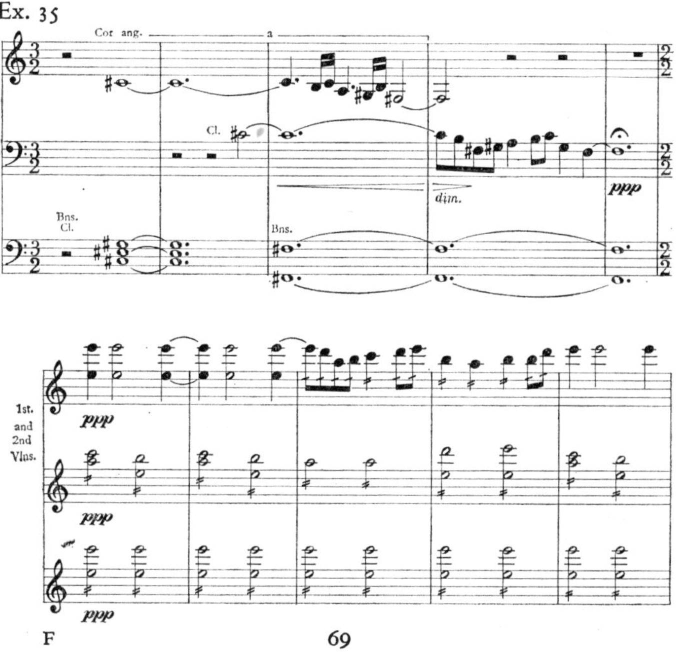

The essential contour of this melody is described with astonishing simplicity within the compass of a perfect fifth and, like most of the ideas in this *Legend*, and in fact much of Sibelius's other music of this period, studiously flattens the leading note. This is true of the *Ballade* from the *Karelia* music, *Lemminkäinen's Return*, *Nightride and Sunrise* and *Pohjola's Daughter*.

What distinguishes *Lemminkäinen in Tuonela* from the other *Legends* is its use for dramatic effect of direct tonal contrasts: in no other symphonic poem is this so pronounced. The resumption of the material of the first section takes place without the remotest preparation (bars 276–7) and the effect is no less striking than the example quoted above. The closing pages of the work, too, are characteristic of the tonal ambiguity that Sibelius likes to leave with his listener here: it is by these means, and the dark, sombre orchestral colouring, that Sibelius evokes so powerfully the atmosphere of the legend.

Lemminkäinen's Return tells how the hero, having been released from Tuonela with the remnants of his body sewn together by his mother's magic charms, makes his journey homeward. Sibelius fuses two separate episodes in the *Kalevala* which relate all the excitement that surrounds Lemminkäinen's progress as he gallops furiously through the wild forest landscape of the Northland. The piece is an exciting *moto perpetuo*: the opening three-note figure is a kind of seminal motive that fertilizes all the subsequent thematic material. A great deal of physical excitement is generated by means of the insistent *ostinati,* and sustained semiquaver activity. Though none of the modulations is comparable in dramatic effect to those of *Lemminkäinen in Tuonela*, they do serve by means of their frequency (the rate of key change is naturally higher) to strengthen the illusion of a journey through constantly changing terrain. This is reinforced when, at the end of the work, which began in C minor, the colours brighten and the last part takes place in E flat major: one feels the terrain is a welcoming one. Some of the *ostinati*[1] are reminiscent of those in *En Saga* and

[1] Pages 38–41 of the miniature score published by British and Continental Music Agencies Ltd.

those which Sibelius later uses in *Nightride and Sunrise*, a work which is not dissimilar in theme. In their effect, too, the closing bars curiously anticipate those of the first movement of the fifth symphony.

In between the four *Legends* and *Pohjola's Daughter*, in which Sibelius again draws on the *Kalevala*, comes the tone-poem *Finlandia*, written in 1899 and revised the following year. To say that this represents Sibelius's work at a low ebb of both inspiration and taste is, in our day and age, a truism. Feelings of national patriotism, however ardent they may be, hardly present the noblest aspect of mankind: such examples of musical nationalism as Elgar's *Pomp and Circumstance* marches or Tchaikovsky's *1812* overture, to name only two, do not show their composers in a very favourable light. *Finlandia* can certainly be classed with these. Its obvious main tune stirs the same shallow emotions as the corresponding tunes in Elgar's patriotic pieces. This is not to say that *Finlandia* is completely worthless: but it is no more fit to move in the company of the *Legends* or *En Saga*, let alone the later symphonic poems, than Elgar's patriotic pieces are worthy bedfellows of the second symphony or *The Dream of Gerontius*.

The symphonic poems that Sibelius wrote during the present century are among his very greatest works and, incidentally, among the greatest essays in this form. In each of them he brings a completely fresh approach to the symphonic poem; no two are alike in their treatment of the programmatic content or in their musical design. *Pohjola's Daughter* is, in a sense, the most 'representational' of them. It was completed in 1906 after the revision of the violin concerto and before the third symphony. The story tells of another of the great heroes of the *Kalevala*. Väinämöinen is on his way home from the Northland when he meets the beautiful maid of Pohjola. He falls an easy victim to her icy charms, but she declines his pressing appeals to her to join him on his homeward journey. To make an end of his wooing she sets him a series of impossible tasks, such as making a boat from the fragments of her spindle and tying an egg in invisible knots. Väinämöinen sets about these with great determination, but they prove beyond even his magic powers, and he is forced to continue his journey alone.

Of all the symphonic poems *Pohjola's Daughter* follows its programme most closely. The frenzied efforts of Väinämöinen to perform his exploits, his first sight of the maid spinning on a rainbow, his passionate intensity and her derisive laughter all find an echo in the music. Yet, in spite of this close adherence to the story, this is nevertheless the most symphonic of the tone-poems up to this date. The unity of its material strikes the listener most forcibly. The plastic cello theme which sets the mood of the saga, the cor anglais melody which grows out of it, are related in a way which is only paralleled in the symphonies. *Pohjola's Daughter* is an unqualified masterpiece. It is the most ambitious and highly organized of Sibelius's essays in this form that he had attempted up to this time. As an example of programmatic art its achievement is fully commensurate with the finest of the Strauss epic tone-poems like *Don Juan* or *Till Eulenspiegel*, while as pure music it represents a degree of cohesion and integration even greater than Strauss's.

If *Pohjola's Daughter* is not played as often as it deserves in the concert hall, *Nightride and Sunrise*, which followed in 1907,[1] is almost completely neglected. Its comparative unpopularity may well rest on a series of uninspired performances. Unless the cumulative effect of the long first section is realized in performance, the impact of the work tends to be greatly diminished. It is in fact a most exciting piece, every bar of which is characteristic of the composer. At first glance the *ostinati* and the lengthy pedal points suggest that the work belongs more to his early period; indeed, the *ostinati* are of a type that we have already encountered in *Lemminkäinen's Return* and *En Saga*. Here, though, Sibelius makes even more daring use of these devices: they are sustained at greater length and managed with the greater simplicity of real assurance.

Nightride and Sunrise falls roughly into the two sections suggested by its title. The first is almost entirely dominated by a trochaic rhythm, which settles down in E flat, though there are a number of gentle key

[1] A number of authorities, including Ekman and Abraham, date this 1909. This was in fact the date of its first performance in St Petersburg. According to Fru Eva Paloheimo, the composer's eldest daughter, the date of composition was 1907.

shifts during its course. This insistent rhythm well conveys the effect of an endless journey through a changing, shadowy landscape. Sibelius often heightens the tension and mystery by reducing the dynamics to a mere whisper. He holds back the most important thematic idea of the section for a considerable time: the tonality has moved to C minor and over an *ostinato* figure the woodwind give out this stirring motive:

Ex. 36

The trochaic rhythm gives way, almost imperceptibly, when the music moves into G minor. Now the scoring is reversed: the *ostinato* figure is heard on the woodwind while the violins announce the motive *sul* G. The skill with which Sibelius changes from the trochaic *ostinato* to equal semiquavers is no less evident in the transition to the second section of the work. This begins with some very eloquent writing for strings alone. Afterwards Sibelius evokes with music of tremendous power and imaginative intensity the magical changes wrought by the sunrise in these northern latitudes. The simplicity of some of the thematic material serves only to underline the feeling of contact with nature. There is some magnificent writing for brass that adds to the growing warmth of feeling—a warmth, incidentally, that is unusual in Sibelius's later nature music. At the height of their glowing peroration the brass are suddenly interrupted by some chords that in their remote and mysterious beauty provide the most poetic touch in the whole work. Their cool pallor contrasts markedly with the rich E flat colouring of the context.

Nightride and Sunrise has something of the tonal stability that marks off the later symphonic poems from *En Saga* and the four *Legends*. Abrupt key changes become far fewer in the later tone-poems, and, though there are many excursions into related keys, the bulk of the action is played out in the area of E flat, just as for all its periods of uncertain tonality B minor is the basic anchorage of *Tapiola*. There are also many surprising touches of orchestration, including some marvellously splenetic bassoon comments derived from the opening orchestral outburst. Indeed, *Nightride* has many touches of real vision, and it is a pity that it is so seldom heard. Although it cannot match *Pohjola's Daughter* in its compactness of utterance and variety of ideas, any more than it can the profound imaginative intensity of *The Bard* or *Tapiola*, it is nevertheless a very fine piece.

Nightride and Sunrise shares with *The Bard* (1913) the absence of any detailed programme, though a good deal of the former is frankly pictorial. Nothing could be in greater contrast to *Nightride* than this intense and contemplative work, Sibelius's first orchestral piece (apart from the *Scènes historiques*) after the fourth symphony. Whereas *Nightride* is spacious, largely extrovert in feeling with a good measure of orchestral excitement, a number of easily recognizable melodic strands, and a glowing climax in the major key, *The Bard* is by contrast the shortest and most introspective. Its slow pace precludes any of the rhythmic excitement that the *Nightride* offers; its melodic substance is slight and confined in fact to a few gentle wisps of melody. The scoring is for the most part soft and delicate, with a harp playing an important role in the proceedings. But despite its brevity and its static quality *The Bard* is no slight work. Its cryptic thematic utterance matches its slender proportions and intimate musings. Superficially it falls into two parts, but the change in mood between them might well be compared to the shift in emphasis in the second part of a sonnet. Both parts are closely related in feeling, but the second and slightly shorter section raises the emotional temperature a little. However, composure returns with the reassertion of the gentle melancholy of the opening.

The very beginning of the work is full of poetry: the melodic strands from which it is woven are of the greatest simplicity. A descending sequence of chords on the harp and a semiquaver rustle from the violas provide the main substance of the music. The atmosphere evoked is both intense and haunting: it is quite unlike any of the other tone-poems in feeling:

Ex. 37

Although *Luonnotar* is not a symphonic poem in the usual sense of the word (or even the Sibelian unusual sense), it is on too extended a scale to be regarded as a song with orchestra or even a *scena* like *Höstkväll.* Indeed it is quite unlike anything else in music. Original even by Sibelius's own standards, the work bears the subtitle 'tone poem for voice and orchestra'. While in design it is not as subtle or complex as *Pohjola's Daughter* or *The Oceanides*, it is remarkably continuous in feeling. *Luonnotar* is the mistress of the air in Finnish mythology, and the words tell of the story of the creation of the world as related in the first Runo of the *Kalevala.* It seems likely that it was nearing completion as early as 1910, since the first performance of a 'new tone-poem written for the Finnish soprano Aino Ackté' was promised for that year. In the event, however, it appeared only after a further three years, in which the fourth symphony and *The Bard* saw the light of day, when it was given its *première* in Gloucester.

Luonnotar is one of those works that are more often praised than played. It is the most gravely neglected of all Sibelius's greatest works. Its neglect is really not difficult to explain, for the solo part is very exacting: the *tessitura* is extremely wide (from B immediately below middle C right up to C flat above the stave, exactly two octaves) and the vocal writing makes cruel demands on the soloist. The line is often angular: there is an exposed entry (on B double flat above the stave) against an accompaniment consisting of B flat, F, G flat and

D flat, while there are numerous other supported entries ascending to C flat, one of them *pp*. The melodic line shows an uncanny feeling for the language; although one occasionally feels on looking at the score that the writing is instrumental, in performance in the language for which it was intended it sounds perfectly judged. The opening idea is a gentle rustling from the strings (F sharp minor), and the voice then enters with its powerfully chiselled theme:

Ex. 38

The rising figure is an important part of the material; and though there is no opportunity for orchestral development on quite the same scale as in the purely instrumental symphonic poems, this does serve to announce the cries of an ascending minor third one hears from the voice in the development. The secondary idea (in B flat minor) has a harp *ostinato* accompaniment and evokes an atmosphere even stranger than that of *The Bard.* The voice line again seems quasi-instrumental on paper, but once heard in the original language its vocal quality becomes apparent:

Ex. 39

Both these passages are restated, but as is always the case with the symphonic poems the process of development is continuous. Only this second idea is left virtually unchanged. It leads directly into what is perhaps the most mysterious of all Sibelius's codas. *Luonnotar* is a work whose power and intensity are paralleled only in *Tapiola* and *The Bard.*

Unlike the brooding *Luonnotar, The Oceanides* does not draw on the *Kalevala.* It is Sibelius's only tone-poem to evoke the world of Homeric mythology. Although the title of the work is given as *Aallotaret,* Sibelius made it clear that this was but a translation into the terms of the Finnish sagas. The Oceanides were the nymphs that inhabited the rivers, streams and waters of classical antiquity. The work was written for Sibelius's American tour in 1914 and was apparently revised after his Atlantic crossing. The work is far more ambitious and highly organized in design than *The Bard,* and far more dramatic in content. The music is richer in melodic interest and more varied in mood. The greyish, ethereal opening very quickly merges into a much sunnier mood, though the sunlight is of the pale northern variety, all the more exquisite for being so short-lived. The proceedings are punctuated by the opening flute theme, and this lends the work something of the aspect of a free rondo. Towards the end of the piece clouds darken the horizon and the music builds up to a tremendous climax.

Several writers, including Cecil Gray, have commented on its 'impressionism'. Certainly the orchestral layout, with its liquid sounds from the harp and its delicate writing for the strings, produces an effect which differs from any of the previous tone-poems or, for that matter, any of Sibelius's other works up to this time. However, on closer examination *The Oceanides* can be seen to employ the normal Sibelian procedures and techniques. Its growth from the opening bars onward is profoundly organic, and its apparent independence from the rest of Sibelius's work is manifest only at a superficial level.

The Oceanides was the last of Sibelius's tone-poems to be written before the First World War. A gap of almost twelve years elapsed before his last and greatest symphonic poem was finished. It is indeed arguable that *Tapiola* is his greatest single achievement. Already in the thirties Cecil Gray made sweeping claims for it: 'Even if Sibelius had written nothing else, this one work would entitle him to a place among the greatest masters of all time.' There is no doubt that in *Tapiola* Sibelius exhibits the most subtle and complete mastery of symphonic procedure, in the sense that he achieves a continuity of thought paralleled only in the symphonies. *Tapiola* is unique even in Sibelius's output: its world is new and unexplored, a world of strange new sounds, a landscape that no tone-poem has painted with such inner conviction and complete sympathy. Nowhere, except possibly in Debussy's *La Mer* and *Nuages*, is the feeling for nature so intense as to amount to complete identification. Yet though its world is unpeopled and the evocation of the unending sunless forests so powerful, there is, particularly in the closing pages, a longing for human contact.

Tapio is the god of the forest in the *Kalevala*. The score is prefaced by the oft-quoted quatrain which Sibelius himself supplied when asked by his publisher to explain the title:

> Widespread they stand, the Northland's dusky forests,
> Ancient, mysterious, brooding savage dreams;
> Within them dwells the Forest's mighty god,
> And wood-sprites in the gloom weave magic secrets.

The tone-poem is to all intents and purposes monothematic, since the material of the work is nearly all derived in some way or other from the opening theme. It was Ernest Newman who called *Tapiola* a symphony and drew attention to the extraordinary degree of organic cohesion that marks Sibelius's thinking in this work. It is in this important sense, though not in any other, that *Tapiola* can be called symphonic. The usual dramatic interest and contrast of key centres that we associate with the symphony are not in evidence.

Of all Sibelius's work it is *Tapiola* which shows the most profound originality in its handling of the orchestra. The sounds that he draws from what is merely a normal large orchestra without extra percussion or even harp are completely new. No one had ever before made the orchestra sound as it does in *Tapiola*; nor for that matter is so highly personal an utterance susceptible of imitation. All the familiar features of Sibelius's scoring are to be found here: the extraordinarily resourceful and imaginative use of the woodwind, the massive writing for the brass and the cross-hatch writing for the strings. But the demands made on all these are pressed to their uttermost limits, and the invention is inseparable from the instruments to a degree unsurpassed elsewhere in his work. A large amount of Sibelius's music, including the last four symphonies and many of the tone-poems, is so completely identified with the orchestral source of sound that it is impossible to conceive of them in other terms. Of no work is this more true than *Tapiola*. It is this score, too, that exhibits the most thorough-going and imaginative use of the pedal point in all Sibelius. More often than not it is a major second. As in the seventh symphony, we find the same mastery of transition and the same capacity to move simultaneously at two levels of tempo. One such transition is the passage beginning at bar 208 (fig. G) where the eerie scherzo-like exchanges between the wind and strings are accompanied unobtrusively by a pedal point which floats gently forward at a slower tempo (on horns, bassoons and clarinets): it is this slower tempo which by means of Sibelius's subtle alchemy comes to assume the greater importance.

One does not have to have experienced the vast forests of Scandinavia with all their variety of moods, colours and sounds, their immense loneliness, their magic, terror and majesty, for Sibelius's vision in

Tapiola to make its impact. Its greatness communicates itself independently of its extra-musical intentions. Although it is as perfect an evocation of the forest as *La Mer* is of the sea, its greatness lies in its impact in terms of pure music. In its homogeneity, concentration of utterance and intensity of vision it is a masterpiece of the first order.

CHAPTER IX

OTHER ORCHESTRAL MUSIC

ALTHOUGH Sibelius's mastery of the orchestra was not fully attained until the first years of the present century it is clear that right from the very beginning his approach to the medium was astonishingly original. Like most Scandinavian composers—Nielsen, Berwald and Grieg, to name only three—he writes superbly for the strings. This is only to be expected from a composer who was himself a violinist (as was Berwald) and was accustomed in his early years to writing for various string combinations. But it is interesting to watch the growth of his equally original woodwind and brass writing—not to mention the percussion. Few modern composers have made so extensive (and, again, individual) use of the timpani. What is surprising is that his cross-hatch string writing, his woodwind in thirds, the powerful brass chords which immediately drop to *pp* and then gradually swell to *ff*, rarely seem to be mere mannerisms, so organically welded are they into his way of orchestral thinking. It is only when these devices are taken over by lesser composers—Dag Wirén is an example, or (nearer home) Moeran in his symphony in G minor—that they appear as non-organic figures of speech.

During his studies with Goldmark, Sibelius wrote an overture in A minor, and another work, *Scène de Ballet,* dates from about this time. Yet, apart from these and an earlier attempt at an orchestral work on the theme of Macbeth, his first major work, the *Kullervo* symphony, already reveals an extraordinarily personal idiom of orchestral speech. The brass writing is perhaps a little less idiomatic, and there are plenty of examples of unnecessary doubling. The sound is thicker than in later Sibelius; yet, even comparing this with the scoring of such masters of the late Romantic orchestra as Strauss, Elgar and Mahler, there is no doubt that Sibelius's sound is very much his own. Elgar's brass writing in the scherzo of the first symphony is very much less idiomatic than Sibelius's much earlier work.

Most of the well-known works up to the first symphony have come down to us in revised form: *En Saga* and the four *Legends* are obvious cases. Hearing his music played and no doubt benefiting from the advice of Kajanus, Sibelius was able to adjust his scores to produce exactly the effect he wanted. The *Karelia* music (1893) is the very first of the well-known works to which he made no major subsequent alteration. Although its seams are far from invisible, the overture, Op. 10, is an enjoyable piece. The scoring is thicker and at *tuttis* brasher than in the suite, where there is much less doubling, and the balance of the work is somewhat upset by the introduction of the famous tune from the *Intermezzo*. The second group is one of those melodies that were thought at the time to derive from Karelian folk-music. It seems on the surface to relate to the Russian 'Five'; yet both in the rhythmic inflexion of the line and its absence of squareness there is a distinctly Finnish flavour.

The suite itself is a much better work. The opening of the *Intermezzo* with its horn calls over *pp* strings suggests that the lessons of early Wagner had been learned; though there is no feeling that the music is not thoroughly Sibelian. The *Ballade*, too, is a gentle, beautiful piece scored with much greater economy than the overture. Though its profile is less highly defined than that of its companions, its spare pastoral flavour (the modal writing occasionally sounds like Nielsen) makes a splendid foil to the outer movements. The *Alla marcia* is the most popular of the three movements, and rightly so. It has a thunderingly good tune of which one never seems to tire; apart from its robust melody it is excellently proportioned.

Skogsrået (1894) is based on the melodrama, *The Dryad*, Op. 15, for speaker, piano, two horns and strings, but this remains in the obscurity of manuscript. Apart from the *Cassation* for small orchestra Op. 6, which is also unpublished, the other major work before the *Scènes historiques*, *Vårsång* (*Song of Spring*), comes from this same year, 1894. It is difficult to summon up much enthusiasm for this piece, the material of which seems thin and commonplace by Sibelius's standards. The *Scènes historiques*, Op. 25 (1899), were all subsequently revised in 1911, while the second set, Op. 66, was written the following year. The first is arranged from the music to various patriotic tableaux which Sibelius wrote for the press celebrations. The second, according to Harold Johnson, is unconnected with the original score, although Furuhjelm wrote that one of the themes from *At the Drawbridge* came from the third tableau.

The first scene, *All' Overtura*, originally formed part of a tableau which pictured Väinämöinen seated on a rock strumming his *kantele* while the Maiden of Pohjola was to be seen at her golden spinning-wheel in the sky. The work has a neo-classical simplicity of language which anticipates the Sibelius of the third symphony rather than the second, which had yet to be written. Its thematic material is not, however, as striking as that of the *Scena*, a more sombre work cast in a dark key (E flat minor) and again fully characteristic of the mature composer. Designed to accompany the tableau depicting Finland during the Thirty Years War, this seldom-heard piece has many highly dramatic moments in which the mysterious whisperings of the strings are heard:

Ex. 40

A flute figure immediately after this passage is strikingly reminiscent of the third symphony. *Festivo* is the best-known of all the six *Scènes*

historiques, and it is the only piece in which Sibelius employs Spanish rhythms. Taken partly from the third tableau set in the sixteenth-century court of the Swedish governor of Åbo (or Turku), where festivities are in progress, the work has a gay, carefree character. It presumably acquires its Spanish flavouring from the duke's wife, Catharina Jagellonica, and makes use of castanets.

The Chase is undeniably first class. Its powerful opening bars leave no doubt that it is set in a wild Nordic landscape: the horn calls echo one another under menacing, cloud-laden skies. No less characteristic is the way in which the dark textures quickly disperse and give way to an exciting *Allegro* whose sense of sheer physical momentum and exuberance makes one think immediately of *Nightride* and *Lemminkäinen's Return*. The *Love Song*, the second of the later set, gives the lie to those who deny Sibelius's warmth. Horns and bassoons support a beautiful figure on muted violas *divisi*: this is a sustained threnody of great eloquence.

At the Drawbridge is a masterly example of Sibelius's lighter music: it misses perfection only by a few bars, for it would gain immeasurably by being very slightly shortened. Two flutes lead an altogether delightful and often witty woodwind conversation over a sustained *pizzicato* accompaniment from the strings. There is a lightness of touch and texture about this which suggests a sun-filled landscape, and the horizon only darkens at fig. E, a pedal point over which a group of semiquavers on the strings and a questioning oboe and clarinet figure are heard (was this the idea Furuhjelm mentions? In another context it could well assume an Iberian flavour). These clouds gather from time to time, but never succeed in dispelling the atmosphere of lightness and gaiety. It is a pity that Sibelius permits the syncopated horn chords to descend chromatically at fig. J; this crude passage and perhaps the very closing bars are the only blemishes on an otherwise beautifully judged miniature.

If the *Scènes historiques* show us the nature poet that Sibelius has become, the Romance in C major for strings, Op. 42 (1903), belongs to the elegiac, Grieg-like tradition which he so magnificently transcended elsewhere. Even if we agree with Ralph Wood's verdict that 'the string writing is a model of effectiveness and of unextravagant and resourceful variety', the fact remains that the Romance in C is too mild-mannered a work, too lacking in concentration to rank among the finest Sibelius. Although it is vastly superior to the *Andante festivo* for strings (1922), which is given on State occasions in Finland, it lacks the ultimate ounce of poetic intensity that we find in *Rakastava*. *Rakastava* (*The Lover*), Op. 14, extends the elegiac Scandinavian tradition well beyond its highly circumscribed and local boundaries: there is no doubt that it is one of Sibelius's most perfect compositions. To the strings of the Romance in C major Sibelius here adds percussion—timpani in the outer movements and a triangle in the innermost. The thematic substance from which the suite is derived comes from the choral work of the same name written in 1893, settings of poems from Lönnrot's *Kanteletar*. When Sibelius came to rearrange the work a year after it appeared in its original form for male chorus *a cappella* he added strings.

In 1898 he rearranged it a second time for mixed chorus *a cappella* but in 1911 he did a good deal more than merely rearrange. To follow the changes through which *Rakastava* passed would in itself provide a fascinating study of Sibelius's working methods and his feeling for voices. Nobody who was unaware of its origins would imagine that *Rakastava* was not wholly conceived in terms of the strings, so perfectly does it seem to belong to its medium. It would be difficult to place the work in Sibelius's output if one did not know its history. So perfect is its craftsmanship, so unified is each part to the whole, so balanced are the means and the ends, that it could only be by a master who had achieved as much as Sibelius had by 1911; at the same time, the ethos of the music belongs to the early years of his self-discovery and the thematic material has nothing of the brooding introspection of the fourth symphony. Yet as far as his feeling for the medium is concerned there is no doubt that this is as perfect as *Voces intimae*, with which it has more in common than its key. Just as the first movement of that compresses the whole of a subtly masterful sonata drama into a comparatively short time, so *Rakastava* concentrates all its lyrical intensity and dramatic allusion into the most compact of frameworks. The delicacy and tenderness with which Sibelius touches on the feelings of young love with all its poetry, anguish and ecstasy, is indeed far removed from the Gallic conception of him as remote and detached. The melodic substance is of the very highest: yet, as with all Sibelius, it is subtly related to everything else in the music. This touching melody that opens the last movement, *Good Night—Farewell!*:

Ex. 41

seems to arise naturally from a subsidiary figure in the first, *The Lover*:

Ex. 42

There is no more wonderful tune in all Sibelius than that of the exquisitely wrought and moving second movement, *The Path of the Beloved.*

At the present time *Rakastava* seems to have fallen out of the repertory, but one can confidently predict that this state of affairs will not continue, for it is a work of astonishing beauty. The neglect of *In Memoriam* (1909) or *The Dryad* (1910) is less difficult to appreciate. They both belong to that category of Sibelius's compositions that will always (and rightly) provoke division of opinion. *In Memoriam* does not belong to his finest work, yet at the same time to dismiss it as 'a pretentious conflation of the *Eroica* slow movement and the funeral march from *Götterdämmerung* but without the virtues of either'[1] is too easy a course to take and ignores the searching quality of grief that we find in such a remarkably comfortless passage as this:

[1] Ralph Wood in Gerald Abraham's *Sibelius, a Symposium*, page 43.

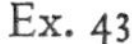
Ex. 43

The angularity and starkness of the bassoon figure almost anticipate Shostakovich. Yet *In Memoriam*, for all its ring of genuine feeling, is not so personal an utterance as one would expect. It seems to have the quality of the sorrow one feels on the death of a well-loved public figure or a favourite writer or artist rather than the loss of a close and intimate friend. But the inexorability of its onward movement, the wave upon wave of descending chromatic lines, and the unrelenting martial rhythms, are not unimpressive.

There are three other smaller works for orchestra written during the years before the First World War: the tone-picture, *The Dryad* (1910), and the *Dance Intermezzo* (1907), which share the same opus number (45), and the seldom-heard *Pan and Echo*, Op. 53 (1906). *Pan and Echo* is a lightweight work lasting a little under five minutes: Sibelius revised it only three years after its composition. While it cannot sustain the same claims on our attention as the *Scènes historiques* or Nielsen's remarkable *Pan and Syrinx*, it is full of quite characteristic material, even though the sense of direction never seems wholly sure. The work modulates quite freely and is frankly sectional much in the same way as the more interesting tone-picture, *The Dryad*. This dates from the same year as the fourth symphony and shares something of its exploratory feeling: indeed one is reminded of the second group of the first movement of the symphony at bars 13–15. What is so surprising about *The Dryad* is the absence of any real continuity of growth. Changes of tempo and substance are legion, and although there are many imaginative touches the work as a whole does not seem to hang together. The *commodo* section at fig. E, for example, does not belong to the same world as the searching opening bars, which are worth quoting:

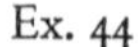
Ex. 44

Here is another instance of the effect of space produced by omitting the inner harmonic support. One of Sibelius's achievements between the third and fourth symphonies was to show that he could work without this 'continuo' support. Mahler was arriving at much the same goal during the first decade of the century: the first episode of the finale of his ninth symphony is a perfect instance of this. *The Dryad* is scored for fairly large forces, though Sibelius takes (for him) the unusual step of omitting the timpani. It can, however, be performed by a smaller *ensemble*.

Its companion piece, the *Dance Intermezzo*, is much less ambitious and far more successful artistically. It is scored for a smaller orchestra (single woodwind, four horns, one trumpet, percussion, harp and strings) and is wholly light in character. It is an instance of Sibelius's more effective writing in this vein: the main theme is not in itself distinguished but (at fig. B) it develops into a most engaging and infectious idea. Even though the *Dance* is marred by an indifferent introduction it is vastly superior to the post-war works like the *Three Pieces* (*Valse lyrique*, *Autrefois*, *Valse chevaleresque*), Op. 96 (1920), the *Suite mignonne* and *Suite champêtre* (1921) and the *Suite caractéristique*, Op. 100 (1922).

Were it not for the evidence of the sixth and seventh symphonies, *Tapiola* and *The Tempest*, one would assume, from the post-war orchestral works in smaller forms, a decline in Sibelius's creative powers. The *Valse chevaleresque* and the *Valse lyrique* pay tribute to Johann Strauss, whose waltzes Sibelius admired all his life; but these specimens lack spontaneity and life, and *Autrefois*, Op. 96b, is no less empty. Perhaps these and the two suites, Op. 98, would arouse more enthusiasm had they appeared at the very outset of Sibelius's career. Indeed, hearing them without any foreknowledge, one would date them as early examples of Sibelius at his most lightweight. Of the two, the *Suite mignonne*, Op. 98a, for flutes and strings is probably the more successful. Both this and the *Suite champêtre* for strings alone, Op. 98b, have come in for a good deal of adverse criticism.

It is true that the first movement, *Petite scène*, of the *Suite mignonne* indulges too readily in sequences, and the way in which Sibelius prepares the entry of his main theme, in itself cheap, is unworthy of his mastery. In fact this movement is, by his standards and even accepting his modest aims, a piece of hack jobbery. There is, however, genuine merit in the second movement, the *Polka*. This is a delightful piece very much in the style of a dance number from a Tchaikovsky ballet. It is in itself interesting that one should be reminded of Tchaikovsky at so late a stage, and although it would be idle to pretend that it is Sibelius's best light music (it is certainly not comparable with the Entr'acte from *Pelléas*, for example), it is definitely appealing. It is a pity that the middle section is inferior and that the return to the main key is managed so clumsily. The opening movement of the *Suite champêtre* is Tchaikovskian both in its rhythmic pattern and harmonic flavouring: it hardly justifies its title of *Pièce caractéristique*.

The *Mélodie élégiaque* is more obviously Scandinavian in feeling but it seems to be written without real conviction or sense of purpose. The opening idea of the final *Danse* is characteristic—indeed it almost reminds one of the *Humoresques*—but the remainder even of this tiny movement does not live up to its promise.

Nor can the *Suite caractéristique* for harp and strings, Op. 100, inspire much enthusiasm. The *Andante festivo* for strings (1922) is also indifferent Sibelius, though his authorship is never in doubt. It is a solemn piece whose eloquence is that of an official national mouthpiece rather than that of the seer of *Tapiola*. Oddly enough, one or two of its phrases are reminiscent of 'God Save the Queen'.

CHAPTER X

MUSIC FOR THE THEATRE

ONE feature of the contemporary musical scene is the decline and debasement of light music. The eighteenth-century composer poured out functional music of this kind in great profusion; and although the collapse of the aristocratic order and the rise of a newly enriched *bourgeoisie* undermined standards of taste in light music, composers like Dvořák and Brahms could turn their hand to light music in a way that is largely foreign to the twentieth century. There are exceptions: Poulenc, Ibert and Françaix have written light music of great elegance. None of them, however, has written the substantial symphonic works that Elgar and Sibelius have; nor have any of their lighter pieces gained the wide currency of *Valse triste* or *Salut d'amour*. Light music nowadays is almost exclusively the preserve of the specialist, who is geared to meet the constantly changing needs of a market artificially stimulated by the demands of the mass media.

Although his symphonies evince the highest quality of organic thought, Sibelius could think in the simplest musical terms and write in a comparatively light idiom. Pieces like *The Oak-tree* or the *Chorus of the Winds* from *The Tempest* are fired with an imaginative intensity worthy of the best Sibelius, yet they are essentially 'pattern' music: it is this kind of musical thinking that is the very stuff of light music. Most of his incidental music is a good deal lighter than the rest of his orchestral output, and even the best, such as *The Tempest*, contains music so light that it seems in positive danger of taking off altogether.

No reminder is necessary of the importance of the theatre in nineteenth-century Scandinavia as a forum for new ideas. Ibsen, Strindberg and Björnson are evidence of its extraordinary vitality at this time. The Scandinavians take the theatre seriously and there is hardly a composer of note who has not written for the stage. Sibelius wrote incidental music for eleven productions altogether, though not all of them call for a large orchestra. The first play for which he provided music was *King Christian II* by the Swedish dramatist Adolf Paul. This play was a great success at the time, though it has since disappeared from the repertory, leaving only the music to hold the public. The plot concerns the love of Christian II, whose dominion extends over all three Scandinavian countries, for a Dutch girl called Dyveke, who is a commoner. The famous *Musette* was intended in the production to be danced by her.

According to Paul, Sibelius said:

> It should be for bagpipes and reeds, but I've scored it for two clarinets and two bassoons. Extravagant, isn't it? We have only two bassoon players in the entire country, and one of them is consumptive. But my music won't be too hard on him—we'll see to that.

This is a concrete reminder of the limited orchestral resources open to Sibelius at the time. He himself conducted the small *ensemble* consisting of two flutes, two clarinets, two bassoons, harp and strings, which were all placed behind the scenes. To the four movements that make up the original music—the *Elegy* for strings which prefaced the play, the *Musette*, the *Minuet* and the *Fool's Song*—Sibelius was encouraged to add three for larger forces—*Nocturne*, *Serenade* and *Ballade*. This suite was his first orchestral work to appear in print, and introduced him to both the German public and the Anglo-Saxon world. It reached Leipzig in 1898, its year of composition, and Henry Wood introduced it in this country at the 1901 'Prom' season.

Like the *Karelia* music written some five years before, *King Christian II* belongs to the *genre* of Scandinavian national-romanticism, but in its quality of inspiration it moves on a much lower level. The *Karelia* music undoubtedly presents a far more individual profile. The *Elegy*, beautiful though it is, is not far removed in spirit from the eloquent Grieg miniatures like *Heart's Wounds* and *The Last Spring*. The *Minuet* and the *Fool's Song of the Spider* are conventional pieces with comparatively little individuality: it is the *Musette*, gently playful and a trifle naïve, that is the most characteristic piece. Only the bars that return the middle section to the main idea seem unworthy of the composer. The three other movements, which are scored for a larger orchestra of double woodwind, four horns, two trumpets, three trombones, timpani and strings, are not first-rate Sibelius. The *Nocturne* has many touches that are unmistakably personal, even though the main idea is not so distantly related to Mendelssohn's *Lieder ohne Worte*. It is one of the few ideas in Sibelius's orchestral music that could well be translated into keyboard terms without doing its nature real violence. The movement has a certain freshness and generosity of feeling, but the seams that join the various paragraphs are clearly visible. Yet for all its immaturity the *Nocturne* has something of the awkward charm of adolescence. Admittedly it is inferior Sibelius, but it is lovable in a sense because of its very faults.

The *Serenade*, which served as the prelude to the third act of the play, likewise has many touches that serve to establish Sibelius's identity without ever revealing his mastery. The big tune (thirteen bars after fig. C) on unison violins is pallid by comparison with the melodic sweep of the first symphony written only a year later. The *Ballade* is a rumbustious piece that is undoubtedly effective within its limits; but if it is put alongside pieces of a similar character such as *The Return of Lemminkäinen* and *Festivo*, or for that matter the finale of the symphony, to which there is a very superficial resemblance in places, its inadequacy becomes readily apparent.

If the *King Christian II* suite was the first orchestral work by Sibelius to make its way into the concert halls of Europe, his next essay in the realm of the theatre was destined to make his name a household word. This was the music to *Kuolema (Death)*, a play by his brother-in-law Arvid Järnefelt. In the opening scene the central character, Paavali, is seen at the bedside of his dying mother. She tells him of her dream that she has gone to a ball. Later, while Paavali himself sleeps, Death comes to claim her and the mother, mistaking him for her dead husband, dances with him. When Paavali wakes up his mother is dead. It is in this context that *Valse triste* began the long life that took it into the tea-shops of Europe and America. It is difficult to imagine the effect this seductive piece made on its first appearance, so hackneyed has it become. It is associated now with so many improbable instrumental combinations that one tends to lose sight of the fact that it is an original miniature, despite the obviousness of some of its musical procedures. The middle section is commonplace by the side of the main idea.

The rest of the music to *Kuolema* is relatively obscure. Some of it cannot be transplanted into the concert hall, since it consists of simple musical devices designed purely to invoke a background mood. Two years after the production was first staged in 1904 Sibelius revised two scenes for concert use. These he called *Scen med tranor* (*Scene with cranes*), an evocative piece for clarinet and strings. Two other pieces were published in 1911: the *Canzonetta* for strings, Op. 62a, and the *Valse romantique* for small orchestra, Op. 62b. In the rarely played *Canzonetta* the strings are muted throughout and the music has some of the wistful, alluring melancholy of *Valse triste.* The sequences in the paragraph beginning at fig. A are particularly reminiscent of that famous piece. It is beautifully laid out for the strings and has far greater distinction altogether than its companion, the *Valse romantique.* This is scored for two flutes, clarinet and horns, timpani and strings, and is frankly a *salon* piece with little real vitality to commend it.

Most of Sibelius's important music for the stage, apart from *The Tempest*, dates from the middle of the first decade of the present century. Hot on the heels of *Kuolema* came scores for *Pelléas et Mélisande* (1905), *Belshazzar's Feast* (1906) and *Swanwhite* (1908). Of these it is the music for *Pelléas* that is best known. This is a magnificent score, even though Sibelius does not quite capture the mystery and the sultry crepuscular atmosphere of Maeterlinck in the way that Debussy and Fauré do. There is a distinct northern accent about the music: the lines are clear-cut, the colours are of great pallor and delicacy, yet he does not fully enter Maeterlinck's world.

The suite that Sibelius prepared for concert purposes consists of nine movements. Though few of them are as highly personal or inward-looking as the music for *The Tempest*, they are distinguished by immense polish and attractive thematic ideas. The best of them, the glorious *Pastorale* and insistent, menacing *Mélisande at the Spinning-Wheel*, are as good as anything Sibelius wrote in this *genre*. The others strike a less profound imaginative vein: the opening movement, for example, falls back too readily on conventional Sibelian rhetoric for it to be a worthy bedfellow of the *Pastorale*. If *At the Castle Gate* seems somewhat forced, *Mélisande* is another matter: although it is a trifle facile, the cor anglais melody that dominates it has a grave charm that seems to spring from a more spontaneous creative impulse. The third number, *At the Seashore*, runs to some twenty-two bars and serves the purely functional purpose of evoking atmosphere. Its characteristic but by no means distinguished matter is held together over a pedal-point. *By a Spring in the Park* is, like *Mélisande*, a wholly successful piece of pattern music which has no pretensions to any kind of musical development. The main tune is characteristic of the way in which Sibelius avoids the obvious. Many composers would have omitted the sixth bar in the interest of a well-balanced eight-bar phrase: Sibelius's melody fascinates because of its very asymmetry:

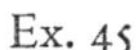
Ex. 45

The Three Blind Sisters is a touching, strophic song of disarming simplicity. As it stands in the suite (the melodic line is allotted to the cor anglais) its pathos provides an admirable foil to the *Pastorale* which follows. The latter is one of Sibelius's most perfect miniatures: its luminous scoring evokes the delicacy of colouring of the gentle northern summer, and the lightness of texture almost suggests that the music was conceived *en plein air*. *Mélisande at the Spinning-Wheel* is of a similarly high order of imagination. The writing for the violas is onomatopoeic in function, as is that for the oboe, with its descending three-note chromatic figure, and the clarinets, whose halting melody admirably conveys the irregularity of the wheel's motion. The *Entr'acte* is another superbly designed, unpretentious movement. Its mood is sunny and life-giving: the sense of movement generated by the quaver motion never ceases and the melodic line has a logic and sense of direction that seem almost classical. This is the kind of polished miniature which, because of its divertimento-like nature, is apt to be underrated even by the connoisseur of Sibelius: it radiates sheer joy in music-making. The *Death of Mélisande* is a beautiful piece too, though it is clearly related to the conventional Scandinavian elegiac style.

Sibelius's music to *Belshazzar's Feast*, a play by his friend Hjalmar Procopé, is by no means as well known as *Pelléas*. Yet it is a score of great quality. The play concerns the intrigues at the court of Babylon and is apparently of little interest; in fact one cartoonist at the time showed Procopé being held aloft by Sibelius. The suite that Sibelius drew up from the music is rarely heard in the concert hall, and has only once been recorded (but that magnificently in the early thirties by Kajanus) so that *Belshazzar* is hardly known even to the Sibelius enthusiast. In a sense it is typical of the incidental music in that it follows a pattern formula and makes no pretence at development. Yet, despite its disarming simplicity, and indeed perhaps because of it, it has a poetic effect of great intensity. Least successful is the opening *Oriental March*, where the attempt to evoke the colours and atmosphere of an Eastern procession is greatest. This repetitive piece is no doubt effective in its theatrical context, but barely justifies its place in the concert hall. The other pieces are a totally different matter. *Solitude*, with its undulating whispered string *ostinato*, is a most poetic and affecting piece of outstanding beauty, and *Night Music* is no less searching and inspired. The last number of the suite is *Khadra's Dance*, an exquisite little piece of a cool, fresh charm, punctuated by this haunting, affectionate oboe melody:

Ex. 46

As with many of Sibelius's slighter works, *Belshazzar's Feast* can easily be spoilt by a performance that falls short in imagination or affection; its delicacy and poetry are elusive.

Swanwhite is another Sibelius score that is more praised than played. It makes a very considerable impact when heard in the context of Strindberg's play. From the fourteen scenes that comprise the full score the composer made a suite of seven pieces. They are not as immediately striking or attractive as the music to *Pelléas*, nor have they the compelling atmospheric vein of *Belshazzar*. Indeed, like *Nightride and Sunrise*, *Swanwhite* is slow in surrendering its secrets and has a less sharply defined profile than its immediate neighbours. It is by no means even. The first number, *The Peacock*, is characteristic Sibelius in that it bears his fingerprints clearly enough, but its invention is by no means of the highest quality. Nor is the finale, *Hymn of Praise*, more than partially successful: the imaginative intensity of its opening is not really maintained, and the close (from fig. C onwards) seems comparatively lame and unresourceful. Best known is *The Maidens with Roses* (its title, *Tärnorna med rosor*, is sometimes inaccurately rendered as *The Maiden with the Roses*), an alluring, lightly scored piece which runs to no more than sixty-six bars. It has something of the same seductive quality as *Valse triste*, though it does not have the pronounced *salon* flavouring of its middle section. Only three of the movements are first-class Sibelius: *Listen, the Robin Sings* is an imaginative piece, and its opening provides an interesting and novel variant of the beginning of *La Chasse*, or the first of the four *Legends*. The texture has a space and freedom that recall the beautiful *Pastorale* from *Pelléas*. *The Prince Alone* is an eloquent piece, much tauter and more intense in feeling; the modal shape of the melodic line is not dissimilar to *Nightride and Sunrise*, which dates from much the same time. This and *Swanwhite and the Prince*, the most immediately beguiling of all the movements, have a continuity of ideas and a simplicity of utterance that set them apart from the others.

There are four other scores for the stage before *The Tempest*: first, to Mikael Lybeck's *Ödlan* (*The Lizard*) (1909); second, to Adolf Paul's *Language of the Birds* (1910); third, to Poul Knudsen's pantomime, *Scaramouche* (1913); and lastly, to Hofmannsthal's *Everyman* (1916). Interest was roused in the first of these when Sibelius wrote in a letter quoted by Ekman that this score was 'among the most full of feeling that I have written'. He began work on it after his return from England in 1909 and completed it by the October of that year. The play was not, however, successful when it appeared the following year and was taken off after only six performances. Scored for a small group of strings (Sibelius asked for nine players if possible, though agreed to a minimum of six), the music runs to forty-three pages of score; the first of the two sections consists of some thirty-seven bars in which the solo violin has an important role. The second is for the third scene of Act II; according to Rosas,[1] this is far more than a routine example of incidental music.

The Lizard bears the opus number 8, but Sibelius did not attach enough importance to Paul's *Language of the Birds* to number it at all. Apart from the *Wedding March*, there is apparently little extended writing of any moment. The music to Knudsen's *Scaramouche*, on the other hand, is on a much more ambitious scale. It is a continuous score which runs to seventy pages even in short score. Some of the ideas from the love scene give the impression that Sibelius is looking back to the world of the second symphony; others confirm Ralph Wood's impression that it is Straussian. The B flat *Allegretto* theme from the love scene is typical of Sibelius's light music from *Valse triste* to later works like the *Suite champêtre*. While *Scaramouche* is an extended work, though of uneven quality, the music to *Everyman* consists of sixteen numbers, some of which comprise only a few bars or are even confined, in the case of the first, to one chord: like *Swanwhite*, it is uneven. The *Allegro* that comprises the third number has considerable delicacy and lightness of touch (its material is more fully developed in the tenth section) but on the other hand the simplicity of the fourth, a strophic song of greeting to Everyman, is not wholly convincing. Most evocative is the eleventh section, which accompanies the spoken dialogue between Everyman and Good Deeds. Here the writing is quite bold: chromatic wisps of sound weave a texture of subtle mystery.

Ex. 47

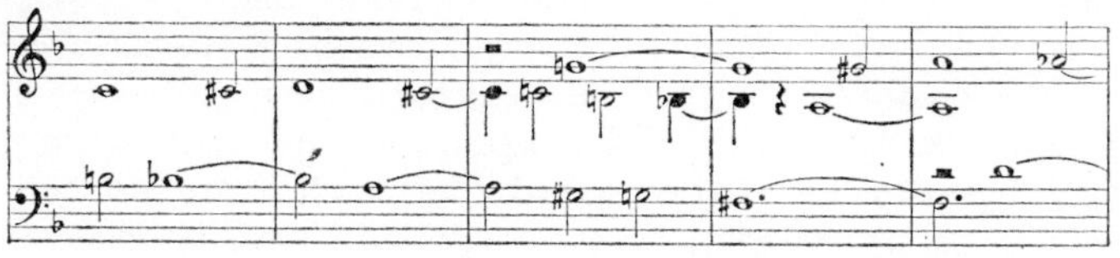

[1] John Rosas, 'Sibelius' musiken till skådespelet, Ödlan' (*Suomen Musiikin Vuosikirja*, 1960–1).

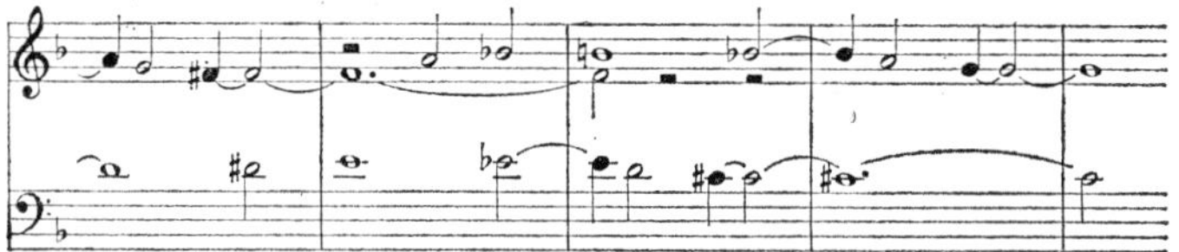

No. 14 contains an unusual stroke of colour: its opening bars are scored for the somewhat bizarre combination of piano, organ and strings.

Sibelius's last and greatest work in this *genre* is the music for the Copenhagen production of *The Tempest* in 1926. Here he was able to use much larger orchestral resources than in any of his earlier music for the stage though, oddly enough, on the title pages he calls it 'a small orchestra'. There is a sense in which it could be said to be among the most uneven of Sibelius's dramatic scores, for the finest pieces, like the *Oak-tree* or the *Intrada and Berceuse*, are on so high a level of inspiration that the less inspired movements are thrown into greater relief. *Miranda* and *Caliban* are on a much lower plane, and it is difficult to reconcile them with the strange other-worldly vision of the *Chorus of the Winds*. In its entirety[1] the *Prelude* must be accounted one of the most effective and terrifying 'storms' in all music. Its effect is achieved by the quality of the texture alone, for it contains almost no passage of real musical development. It consists merely of a succession of rising and falling augmented fourths for the strings, chromatic figures in the woodwind, menacing brass entries and so on. Ralph Wood aptly calls it 'the most thoroughly onomatopoetic stretch of music ever written'. This is no overstatement: the surging seas, strange distant lights and howling gusts of wind (horns, percussion) make an almost physical impact. It is a piece of the utmost virtuosity, and as sheer tone-painting is extraordinarily powerful.

One of the most hauntingly beautiful of the other pieces is *The Oak-tree*. The means it employs could hardly be more simple, yet the music is profoundly original. An anguished flute line moves over an

[1] In the second suite Sibelius included a shortened version of the *Prelude*, omitting the impressive closing pages and ending the piece abruptly (and less effectively) on a chord of E flat minor.

eerie, insistent rocking *ostinato* figure which periodically changes position to great effect:

Ex. 48

A pedal D is either heard or implied throughout the piece (its effect in its absence is no less extraordinary than its re-entries in providing subtle harmonic colouring); its persistence as well as the harmonic course the music takes at the very end of the piece is worth study. The piece is obviously inspired by the plight of Ariel, imprisoned by a witch for twelve years in an oak tree and threatened with like punishment by Prospero. The *Humoresque*, probably associated with Trinculo, belongs to the category of light music: its predictable (or almost predictable) tune has an underlying note of menace which, though never really strong enough to disturb its equanimity, is nevertheless present.

Both *Caliban's Song* and *The Harvesters* belong to Sibelius's lighter vein, though the percussion writing in the former (particularly the xylophone part) seems a trifle out of character and just a little strained. Sibelius did not think naturally in this kind of colouring, and in his attempt to convey the unpolished exterior and awkward gait of Shakespeare's character he forces a bizarre vein that seems unnatural to him. If one did not know its date one would be tempted to place the *Canon* along with the *Historical Scenes*: it has the exuberant classicism of middle-period Sibelius. The *Scene* is a charming C major dialogue between wind and *pizzicato* strings, lightweight but

'AINOLA', SIBELIUS'S VILLA AT JÄRVENPÄÄ

admirably suited to its purpose, for its character is not so highly defined that it draws attention to itself. It is however the *Intrada* and *Berceuse* that strike a deeper vein: the searing dissonances of the former subside after a mere half-dozen bars. These originally served to introduce Act IV in the original production, while the lullaby, a piece of grave and eloquent beauty, is designed for Act I, Scene ii, where Miranda sleeps. It is scored for two clarinets, harp and muted strings. Even if in character it suggests the dark black waters of the river of Death rather than an innocent lullaby, it is a movement of such rare magic and fantasy that it must be numbered among Sibelius's most inspired shorter pieces in any form. It could hardly be simpler in structure: set in E flat minor, a sombre enough key in all conscience, it consists of a melody whose phrases are punctuated by harp arpeggios thus:

Ex. 49

The *Chorus of the Winds* consists of a few sustained chords that do not look particularly impressive on paper, though their effect in performance is spellbinding. These wisps of chords of the seventh with their delicate colouring of woodwind and horns, the gentle wash of muted strings and harp harmonics, produce a sound that is as magical and haunting as it is individual. The E flat minor *Intermezzo* into which it leads returns us to earth. Neither the *Intermezzo* nor the charming *Dance of the Nymphs* has the rapt, breathless quality of the *Chorus*, though they are fine pieces for all that. The character portrait of Prospero is another of the inspired movements; its slow chordal writing has a Purcellian grandeur, but despite its assumption of Restoration trappings and its attempt at pastiche this could only be by Sibelius. As a study of Prospero, it is far more penetrating than the Miranda which we are given later in the same suite. There is a seductive quality about *Miranda*: the opening bars are very promising and the accompanying triplets are a telling stroke. But, alas, Sibelius gives way to a string of sugary sequences which bring unwelcome echoes of the *salon*, unworthy both of the composer and his subject. The remaining pieces, the two songs, the *Naiads*, and the final *Dance Episode* steer a middle course: they eschew the errors of taste we find in *Miranda* but do not attain the level of inspiration that exists elsewhere.

To know *The Tempest* and love it over many years (for all its lapses) compels one to contest Wood's dismissal of the work in his often penetrating essay. Comparing it unfavourably with *Scaramouche*, he writes that 'the Copenhagen commission was a switch that released a cascade of almost exhibitionistic virtuosity at last uncoloured by any tincture of creative impulse'.[1] In the face of the *Intrada* and *Berceuse*, *The Oak-tree*, *The Chorus of the Winds* and *Prospero*, this judgment seems wholly incomprehensible. Here, as is the case with most of his scores for the theatre, Sibelius's poetry and vision far outweigh any of the other reservations we may have about individual pieces. No other twentieth-century composer working in this field has surpassed his achievement.

[1] *Op. cit.*, page 89.

CHAPTER XI

SOLO INSTRUMENT AND ORCHESTRA

WITH the violin concerto (1903, revised 1905) we come to one of Sibelius's most popular yet vulnerable scores. Its popularity undoubtedly springs from the fact that violinists love playing it; it is superbly written (the part bristles with difficulties of the kind players enjoy overcoming) and the music has a *Zigeuner*-like warmth that, like Bruch's G minor, has great public appeal. On this particular level it is a superlative piece and deserves every bit of its popularity. Yet on another it is by no means Sibelius at his best. It is in its failure to live up to the inspired quality of its opening theme—surely a heaven-sent idea and worthy of the composer at his very best—that its crucial weakness lies: and none of the incidental beauties of the rest of the work make up for this. In fact the theme is so superior in quality to the material that succeeds it that it seems a difference almost in kind rather than degree. At the restatement we are reminded of this, and the theme presents the aspect of tarnished innocence. Tovey, it will be remembered, placed this concerto above Mendelssohn's; but that is a work which has a symmetry, perfect homogeneity and a stylistic purity that make it a better work of art. Certainly if no other works survived from their pens but their violin concertos, Mendelssohn's would give us a far more complete picture of its composer and a better idea of his stature than Sibelius's would. But Tovey's opinion is not one that a succeeding generation can lightly set aside:

> Of course the greater concerto form of Mozart, Beethoven and Brahms is another story; instead of being lighter than symphonic form, it is perhaps the most subtle and certainly the most misunderstood art form in all music. But in the easier and looser concerto forms invented by Mendelssohn and Schumann I have not met with a more original, a more masterly, and a more exhilarating work than the Sibelius violin concerto.[1]

---

[1] *Essays in Musical Analysis,* vol. iii (Oxford, 1936), page 211.

Even if it is not one of Sibelius's greatest works, there is much in the score to justify Tovey. Sibelius's grip on his material is as firm as ever. The wistful idea that follows the B flat minor idea (on page 17 of the Eulenberg miniature score) seems to come near to recapturing the high level of poetry that distinguishes the opening. The section beginning at fig. 2, the beginning of the second group in fact, though it is precariously poised between the tonic and B flat, is related to the first theme; the relationship, though obvious enough on paper, is sufficiently natural for the new idea to strike the ear as fresh. Subsequent developments proceed just as naturally. Whether or not one agrees with Wood's strictures on 'the cheap-tragic material' at fig. 3, with 'those plangent flattened melodic thirds and that relapse by the soloist into double-stopped sixths—how effective and how second-rate',[1] one cannot but admire the very continuity of growth that Wood denies it. There is a very real sense of movement: even though the cadenza comes close to the language of the great virtuoso violin composers like Vieuxtemps, Sibelius renders their empty rhetoric far more meaningful. There are, too, flashes of real power in the orchestral writing: the menacing orchestral writing between figs. 5 and 6 is an instance in point: many performances miss the dark strength and intensity of such passages.

The slow movement is considerably weaker. It has a lushness that seems more self-indulgent than any of the more obviously rhetorical gestures of the first. It is interesting to see how Sibelius's use of woodwind in thirds at the opening of the movement has the reverse of its normal effect: far from being cold, the atmosphere evoked is relaxing. Much of the writing in the first group has genuine warmth and nobility. The second idea, on strings, for all its full-bloodedness, is marred by a strange lapse of taste; at its climax (six bars after fig. 1) Sibelius coarsens the line by adding trumpets. The theme at this point momentarily reminds us of the *salon* world to which Sibelius paid ample tribute in the Romance in D flat. For all its undeniable eloquence, this movement is by no means as fine as the slow movements of the first and second symphonies; nor is its inspiration of the quality of *En Saga* or the four *Legends*.

[1] *Op. cit.*, pages 67–8.

If the second is the most soft-centred of the three movements, the finale is undoubtedly the most brilliant and exciting. From the very outset its stunning impetus never slackens. Its rhythm is insistent and the interplay between 6/8 and 3/4 in the second theme is highly effective. It is this with its air of a rather ungainly abandon that brings Tovey's felicitous description to mind, 'a polonaise for polar bears'. The whole finale has an infectious and irresistible sense of momentum, and even in an inferior performance never fails to rivet the attention of an audience.

When we turn to the other music Sibelius wrote for violin, what is striking is not its inferiority but on the contrary the high level of its inspiration. Both the *Serenades* and the *Humoresques* are first-class; only the *Romance*, Op. 78, No. 2, is a straightforward exception. This is an orchestral arrangement of the second of the four pieces, Op. 78, for violin or cello and piano. It strikes an uneasy compromise between the sentimentality of the famous Svendsen *Romance* and the natural breeding and distinction of Stenhammar's *genre* pieces, like the *Sentimentalvals*, without really having any distinct character of its own. The result, at any rate, has the stale pallor of much Scandinavian *salon* music of the period, and is no way comparable in quality with the *Serenades* or the *Humoresques*. The other two pieces Sibelius wrote for this medium, *Cantique* (*Laetare anima mea*), Op. 77, No. 1, and *Devotion* (*Ab imo pectore*), Op. 77, No. 2, both date from 1914 and fall short of the best without going so far as the *Romance*. Indeed, both are considerably more individual, particularly the second. The nobility of the *Cantique* has, however, a conscious rectitude that is reflected in its uneventful line, and it is the second with its searching modulations that is the more interesting. Neither is comparable, though, with the *Serenades* or the *Humoresques*.

What is so striking about these is their totally unforced charm and spontaneity. They have a lightness of touch and a freshness and sparkle that make one wonder why they are not in the repertory of every violinist of standing. Both sets of *Humoresques* date from 1917, the year after the second version of the fifth symphony was completed, and both call for a dazzling technique on the part of the soloist. The first set, Op. 87, comprises two pieces and calls for a small orchestra of double woodwind, two horns, timpani and strings. Of the remaining four, Op. 89, the first two are for strings only, the remaining two include some wind instruments. In these pieces the *Zigeuner*-like virtuosity that we meet in the violin concerto seems to have been wholly absorbed into the composer's stylistic bloodstream. In the second the soloist's part is full of the bustling scale figuration and large leaps we encounter in the violin concerto, but there is much greater delicacy of feeling and gentleness of colouring. The first piece has a similarly haunting flavour, and the writing for the soloist, while no less brilliant than in the concerto, has a far more individual character, as at fig. A for example. The phrase lengths are less predictable, and there is again a sense of onward movement.

The second set is no less fetching than the first. The third of this set has an irresistible tune which once heard is difficult to get out of one's head. This is the most immediately attractive and lovable of the set, and one of Sibelius's most disarming compositions. The first of the Op. 89 has a slightly wistful note of melancholy, and its sighing phrases on muted strings lend it an atmosphere as unmistakable and as difficult to put into words as that of the long still evenings of the Scandinavian summer. Indeed, it is difficult to overpraise these exquisite miniatures; the others are every bit as inventive, and all deserve far more attention than they have been given.

The two *Serenades*, Op. 69, are earlier pieces; in addition to double woodwind they call for four horns, timpani and strings. They are both fine works, full of characteristic touches, though they are perhaps not such perfect miniatures as the *Humoresques*. They are both short, lasting little more than five minutes each. The opening of the first with the modal inflexion it acquires from its flattened seventh, as well as the airy texture, almost suggests Nielsen, though the passage beginning at fig. E could hardly be mistaken for anyone other than Sibelius. The second *Serenade*, in G minor, written a year later in 1913, foreshadows the atmosphere of the *Humoresques*. Apart from the not wholly convincing change into the major in the closing bars, it wears its sad charms with great elegance.

CHAPTER XII

'KULLERVO' AND THE CHORAL MUSIC

THE interest in a composer's early works lies more often in what they have to tell us about his musical inheritance than in their intrinsic merit. Sibelius himself did not think highly enough of the *Kullervo* symphony, his earliest large-scale work, to allow it to be published, even though it was with this work that he made his break-through in Finland. Indeed, he only parted with the manuscript at a time when he was very short of money, and the work had to wait until 1958, the year after his death, before it was heard again in public.

Kullervo is an enormously long work and takes more than an hour and a quarter in performance. Of its five movements, three are purely orchestral, while the third and longest calls for soloists and male chorus. No doubt because of its programme Sibelius shrank from calling it a symphony on the title-page of the score; there he describes it as 'a symphonic poem for soloists, chorus and orchestra'. It is, however, a symphony in much the same sense that Mahler's *Resurrection* symphony can be so described: in other words, it embraces concepts that strictly speaking lie outside the range of the normal classical symphony, though without sacrificing its essentially organic modes of procedure. The work employs comparatively modest resources (there is only double woodwind, for example), since larger forces were not to be had in Helsinki at this time. Its profile is by no means as developed as that of Mahler's symphony; but this is not surprising when we remember that Sibelius was only twenty-six at the time, and that apart from an early overture this was his first serious attempt at writing for the orchestra. Mahler, on the other hand, was seven years older when the *Resurrection* symphony was finished in 1894 and had much greater experience in handling the orchestra, both as a composer and conductor. What is surprising is to find how innate is Sibelius's feeling for orchestral colour. Although his mastery is far from fully developed at this stage, his orchestral writing reflects an astonishing degree of assurance. Kajanus's *Aino* symphony, which Sibelius had heard some months earlier in Berlin, served as an immediate catalyst rather than the model some critics would have us believe. There is never any doubt about its sense of identity.

Like most early works it is clearly derivative in places; the shades of Tchaikovsky are present in the slow movement and the coda of the first. The proportions of the third and fourth movements are far from perfect. Yet what is striking is not so much this debt to the Russians or its formal imperfections as its vividness of personality and the bold sweep of many of its ideas. The very opening of the first movement offers us a magnificent tune over a characteristic ground swell:

Ex. 50

Allegro moderato

Cl. horns

2 Ob.

2 Cl. oct.

Str.

etc.

There is no question of Sibelius's achievement in this movement whatever reservations there may be about the work as a whole. One can well understand the excitement of contemporary critics like Flodin: apart from the individuality of the ideas themselves Sibelius handles the material of this movement with the authority of a master. The sense of forward movement which we know from the mature composer is already evident, and his handling of sonata procedure is confident. The second group opens with a dark horn theme (it reappears in Ex. 51, marked *x*) and maintains the epic mood of the opening. This is less compact than Sibelius's mature melodic thinking, but is already the work of a born symphonist. Here is the passage where it bursts on to the dominant (B minor) with an emphatic *pizzicato* chord:

Ex. 51

The tonal scheme is straightforward but well thought out. The development plunges directly from B minor to E flat minor with dramatic effect. This, and the fact that the keys are (generally speaking) dark, like C minor, help to prepare psychologically for the E major opening of the restatement. In spite of the fact that the seams are clearly visible the continuity of ideas even at this early stage is impressive. One is almost reminded of Bruckner's breadth and sense of mystery at the opening of the development, and certainly of his imaginative use of tonality when the music turns into C minor. The imitative treatment of the main tune produces effects of great spaciousness, and there are many daring and original touches: the quick, repeated B flats on the oboe maintained over a long period is one; another comes at the beginning of the recapitulation, where Sibelius hangs on to a chord of E major for a very long time indeed, the only activity being insistent, repeated *pizzicato* blows. This is highly effective, as is the long, sustained F minor chord at the close of the third movement. The modal flavouring that one finds in early Sibelius is also here: the accompanying figuration at the beginning of the development has a fresh modal quality that reminds one of *Karelia*, or Nielsen. Naturally the corresponding movement of the first symphony has much greater cohesion, and there is no doubt of the enormous strides made by Sibelius in the intervening years, or for that matter in the three or so years which separate this from *The Swan of Tuonela*. The greater compactness of the recapitulation of the first movements of the first and second symphonies is one obvious feature of his growing mastery.

The debt to Tchaikovsky is even more obvious in the second movement, which is subtitled *Kullervo's Youth*, than it is in the unison string theme in the coda of the first. This movement, too, is purely orchestral, and at times offers fleeting hints of a world not far removed from that of the finale of the *Pathetic* symphony. Perhaps the fact that it is in B, hovering between major and minor, reinforces that impression. The main idea, on muted strings. has the tenderness and warmth we find in the slow movement of the first symphony:

Ex. 52

Its pendant is this violin figure which has a folk-like outline:

Ex. 53

Unlike the slow movement of the first symphony, however, this lacks concentration and a sense of direction. This may in some measure be due to the need to convey something of Kullervo's hapless early years (the story is set out in Runos XXXII to XXXIV of the *Kalevala*) and to Sibelius's uncertainty in dealing with symphonic and programmatic elements in the same work. There seems little point-by-point adherence to the events described in the *Kalevala*, and, despite some eloquent string writing, the overall impression left by the movement is somewhat diffuse. One point of interest is Sibelius's use of a whole-tone figure, though there is no tonal ambiguity as there is later in the fourth symphony. This is inherited presumably from the Russian composers of the day, who had in their turn absorbed many of the modal usages of folk-music, including those which give rise to the whole-tone scale.

The opening of the third movement, the longest of the five, anticipates the epic, national strain we find in the familiar *Karelia* music. The movement is called *Kullervo and his Sister,* and deals with the events described in Runo XXXV of the *Kalevala*. The first part concerns Kullervo's attempts to entice a beautiful girl he sees to join him on his journey. The trochaic rhythm conveys the motion of the sleigh to admirable effect later in the movement, though the momentum is nowhere so sustained as in later works like *Lemminkäinen's Return* and *Nightride and Sunrise*. Kullervo's dashing assurance is admirably captured in the opening:

Ex. 54

Allegro vivace

f

It is this central movement that introduces the two soloists, a soprano and a baritone, as well as a male chorus. The choral writing is mainly in unison, only rarely breaking into four parts; sometimes the parallel octaves are thickened by sixths or thirds, but for the most part the chorus is treated with a sturdy simplicity that is by no means ineffective. The setting of the words is fairly straightforward, more often than not syllabic. Most of the sheer excitement and interest of the movement lies in the orchestra, though the soprano's impressive *scena* when the identity of the two characters becomes known and the realization that their relationship is incestuous is apparent, has some dramatic power and makes one wonder whether Sibelius would not have made out very well as an opera composer. After her death, Kullervo's peroration, which abruptly insists on F minor and is punctuated by heavy orchestral *sforzandi,* has an unmistakably Slav ring about it:

Ex. 55

Despite its undoubted *longueurs* and the somewhat stiff choral writing, the third movement is redeemed by numerous imaginative flashes and the intensity of the soprano solo. With the scherzo and finale one feels that what Sibelius is doing here he was very soon to do much better and with greater economy of means in later works. The same is true of the slow movement. The opening of the scherzo, *Kullervo goes to battle*, has the glowing colours and exuberance of *Karelia* and the *Scènes historiques*:

Ex. 56

But on this melody and an attractive later development Sibelius builds far too unwieldly a superstructure. Indeed, his very economy in all his later scherzos may well spring from the excessive length at which this tune is presented.

The finale, *Kullervo's Death*, returns us to the tonic, E minor, but it never really lives up to the imaginative vision of its opening pages. Here Ex. 52 (*x*) appears in the chorus under a string *tremolando*. Subsequently this melody, which Sibelius first introduced in the coda of the first movement, assumes an important role:

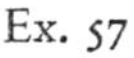
Ex. 57

This idea is fully characteristic of Sibelius's melodic style in his first period, embracing as it does the first five degrees of the minor scale and the flattened sixths. This kind of thinking recurs in *Nightride and Sunrise*, but by then has been fully absorbed into his stylistic blood-stream; here, but more particularly in the coda of the first movement, it has a distinctly Tchaikovskian fervour. In the close of the movement Sibelius refers back to the very opening melody, a far from convincing touch which sounds distinctly contrived. Nevertheless in spite of its miscalculations the *Kullervo* symphony is more than just a work of promise. The fact that a very considerable gulf separates it from the four *Legends* or the first symphony should not be allowed to detract from its achievement. The first movement in particular should be heard, for it speaks with a clear voice and in terms of unmistakable authority.

A glance at the list of works at the end of this volume will show the extent of Sibelius's output for chorus with and without orchestra. Male-voice choirs are very popular in Scandinavian countries, so it is not surprising to find Sibelius writing extensively for this medium. *Rakastava*, one of his most inspired works, began life in this way, and his next choral work, a set of nine part-songs, Op. 18, is also for male chorus *a cappella. Isänmaalle* (*To my country*), the first of them, is typical of the *genre*; patriotic in character with a robust and sturdy melodic line, it serves its purpose admirably. Like the folk-song arrangements or the hymn-tunes of Vaughan Williams, these pieces have solid musical virtues and wide popular appeal. The sixth of the set, *Sydemeni laulu* (*Vale of shadow*), is a beautiful miniature; its line fits the Finnish words like a glove and has great plasticity. These songs all date from the late nineties and the early years of the present century; they continue and extend the tradition of which Pacius is the obvious precursor. It is here that one can speak of Sibelius's relation to an indigenous musical tradition; in no other medium had he any native forbears of serious standing. A similar piece, though with instrumental accompaniment and the relief of boys' voices to take the edge off the high tenor line, is *Atenarnes sång* (*Song of the Athenians*), the third of a set including *Laulu Lemminkäiselle,* a Finnish text, and *Har du mod?*, a Swedish, which comprises Op. 31.

The patriotic flavour of some of these smaller pieces has an echo in the larger choral and orchestral works. The majority of these are difficult of access; the cantata for the University Ceremonies of 1894, the cantata for the Coronation of Nicholas II for soloists, chorus and orchestra (1896),[1] and the Ceremonial Cantata, Op. 23 (1897),[2]

[1] Not 1895, according to Johnson, though previously all other authorities, including Solanterä, Abraham and Ekman, accepted this date.

[2] For soloists, chorus and orchestra, not merely chorus as listed in Abraham. The text is by Forsman. This is the Swedish form of the poet's name. In Finnish he is known as Koskimies.

remain in the obscurity of manuscript. A good deal of this kind of music can be assumed to be primarily functional, though Sibelius thought highly enough of parts of Op. 23 to publish some part-songs which are student songs of good quality. Before we reach *Tulen synty* (*The Origin of Fire*), alternatively known as *Ukko the Firemaker*, there are three works for speaker, chorus and orchestra: *Sandels*, Op. 28, written in 1898 and revised at the time of the fifth symphony, *Islossningen i Uleå älv* (*The Breaking of the Ice on the Uleå River*), Op. 30, dating from the same year, and *Snöfrid* (to words of Rydberg) written in 1896 (not 1900 as listed by Johnson). It is for the most part conventional first-period Sibelius of little distinction.

The Origin of Fire (1902) is a much finer piece. Written for the opening of the National Theatre in Helsinki, it tells how Louhi hides the sun and moon in a mountain and steals the fires from the homes of Väinölä. News of this reaches the chief of the gods in the Kalevala, Ukko, who searches for them in vain. We hear then how he created fire and light and subsequently gave them into the precarious safe-keeping of the Maiden of the Air, who promptly dropped them. The text follows Runo XLVII of the *Kalevala*. The work falls into two sections: the first cast for baritone and orchestra; the second for chorus and orchestra. The latter begins at the point when Ukko forges light and fire from his sword. There is an impressive peroration, though the choral section as a whole is comparatively uninspired—the E minor tune does not show Sibelius at his best. However, there is some good first-period Sibelius in the opening section (see page 116). In any event this is vastly superior to *The Captive Queen*, Op. 48 (1906), a setting of a German translation of Cajander. The theme is patriotic; the queen is Finland and the captor Tsarist Russia, while the atmosphere is undoubtedly redolent of the second symphony. The theme faintly recalls the second group of the finale of the symphony and the cello figure at bar 25 offers another reminder of the same work.

A good many of Sibelius's choral works sound a patriotic note; his special relationship with the Finnish authorities, who contributed to his upkeep, as well as a natural desire to meet the wishes of those commissions he received, might well inhibit his stylistic freedom. In

Ex. 58

the symphonies and symphonic poems he was free to allow purely musical considerations to predominate; and in the solo songs we see how his musical imagination responded to words in a way that is sometimes bold and daring. He maintained his steady output of choral pieces of various dimensions throughout his life: it is only natural, too, that with the coming of independence he should compose on a patriotic theme as in *Oma maa* (*Our own land*), Op. 92 (1918). The flow of occasional pieces continued: *Jordens Sång* (*Song of the Earth*) was written for the inauguration of the Swedish Academy at Turku (Åbo) the following year, and in 1920 he produced *Maan virsi* (*Hymn to the Earth*), Op. 95, to Finnish words. We find that he returns to an earlier style when he deals with the chorus: his writing for voices in no way reflects the ground he has won elsewhere. This may have been due to indifference, to the absence of first-class choirs, or perhaps because he felt some compunction about providing work beyond the capacity of his patrons. Certainly, if *Maan virsi* is typical, the neglect of the choral music outside Finland is understandable. The work begins in a characteristically dark and sombre fashion, but the promise of the opening is not maintained. As soon as the music shifts into the major the writing becomes commonplace.

A PAGE OF THE MANUSCRIPT OF THE FIRST MOVEMENT OF THE 'KULLERVO' SYMPHONY (1892)

(Reproduced by courtesy of Helsinki University Library)

Väinön virsi (*Väinämöinen's Song*), Op. 110 (1926), is an altogether finer piece, though even here the choral writing, to judge from the vocal score, particularly in the first section between figs. C and G, strikes the listener as differing remarkably little from the *Kullervo* symphony. The choral writing is often in unison, or simply two-part, and dark in quality:

Ex. 59

Even when it is in four parts it is frankly homophonic. Admittedly the writing in *Maan virsi* is at one point more contrapuntal, but for the most part it would seem that Sibelius tends to avoid elaborate choral polyphony. For all his admiration of Lassus and Palestrina, the fact remains that there is no living tradition of sixteenth-century music in Scandinavia (outside Denmark), even though the choral works of the great Flemish masters were known and sung in the main Swedish centres and in Åbo. Scandinavia produced no master during the Renaissance: hence their choral tradition is of a simpler kind.

CHAPTER XIII

THE SONGS

WERE only the songs to survive from Sibelius's pen, we should gaina comparatively incomplete picture of him, with but a few glimpses of his real personality and stature. When one thinks of Sibelius's extraordinary powers of compression, his ability to evoke a mood by the most economical of gestures, as well as his highly developed sense of line, one would expect his songs to reflect a mastery comparable with that of orchestral works like *The Bard*. Some of them do; and that strange masterpiece, *Luonnotar*, half song with orchestra, half symphonic poem with vocal *obbligato*, is evidence of a highly original approach to the voice. Yet the most original side of him, as evinced in *Luonnotar*, rarely emerges in the songs. When it does, as in *Höstkväll* (*Autumn Evening*) or *Jubal*, it is in response to nature imagery. And it is in these songs that the larger canvas he employs enables his melodic line to soar with a greater boldness and individuality than we find in the majority of his songs.

Generally speaking, Sibelius's powers of musical compression in the songs are not paralleled by the kind of psychological concentration and range of mood that we find in the quasi-symphonic epigrams of Wolf, or the vivid characterization and intense and often heart-rending humanity of Mussorgsky. Nor is he entirely happy within the confines of the miniature, though this is not to deny that there *are* perfect miniatures among the songs; *Souda, souda, sinisorsa* (*Swim, duck, swim!*) and *Lastu lainehilla* (*Driftwood*) are two obvious examples. Perhaps the most important factor limiting the heights which he could scale is his uncertain keyboard writing. His imagination was in some way inhibited by the piano; rarely does his keyboard writing comment on the vocal line with the freedom one finds in Schumann or Wolf. Even his own countryman, Yrjö Kilpinen, a composer of much more modest stature and an altogether less commanding personality, has a vastly superior sense of dramatic keyboard writing. But Kilpinen is more concerned with the human condition than Sibelius (e.g. *Lieder um den Tod*), and the whole of his talents were concentrated into this medium in a way which is foreign to Sibelius's genius. If man's relationship with nature is the springboard of Sibelius's inspiration in his finest songs, it follows that the orchestra is the desirable (and often essential) means of fulfilment.

It is in the great nature songs that Sibelius's mastery emerges, and he evokes a world totally his own; but even in the songs that do not achieve quite the same heights of inspiration there is ample evidence that his contribution has been underrated. It is only natural that it should be, since the symphonies and symphonic poems are bound to overshadow them. The language barrier, too, stands in his way just as it has in the case of a much greater song-writer, Mussorgsky. Hence the public is familiar with a handful of songs that are not always his very best and are often encumbered with inferior piano accompaniments.

While most of his part-songs are to Finnish texts, the vast majority of his songs for voice and piano are settings of poets writing in Swedish. His very first attempt in the medium was a setting of Runeberg's *Serenade* (1888), but his first important song is *Flickans Årstider* (*The Maiden's Seasons*), sometimes simply called *Arioso* (Op. 3). Again the words are by Runeberg, a poet to whom he was greatly drawn in his youth and to whom he constantly returned for inspiration. *Arioso* has the grave air of melancholy that distinguishes the elegiac Grieg, and much the same intentness and conviction. Written in 1893, the year after the *Kullervo* symphony and *En Saga*, it does not stray outside the Scandinavian tradition. Sibelius also arranged it for strings and revised it in 1912, which accounts for its assurance and polish. It is, needless to say, beautifully laid out for strings and, as is nearly always the case, far more effective than in the piano version. The setting of the words is totally free from artifice: in fact the opening words are given almost equal stresses. There is a touching directness of utterance about this music; there is a hint too of the wide-ranging vocal writing one finds in *Luonnotar*:

Ex. 60

The seven Runeberg settings, Op. 13, which in point of fact precede the *Arioso*, include the well-known *Våren flyktar hastigt* (*Spring is flying*). This is a beautiful little song; its flexible, pliable phrases suggest the transience of the short-breathed seasons. As is so often the case, its effect is greatly enhanced in Sibelius's orchestral version made in 1914. The opening figure, for example, breathes so much more naturally in this version (two flutes, four horns, percussion and strings) that the transformation is beyond the fingers of the most sensitive pianist to convey. The rapid changes of mood are well brought off, despite the brevity of the song, though the more settled it became in E flat the more it tends to be conventional. The very first song of the set, *Under strandens granar* (*Under the fir-trees*) also cries out for orchestral colour. The piano accompaniment consists largely of dark *tremolandi* in the bass clef that spring from the same world of fantasy as *Lemminkäinen in Tuonela* and the *Kullervo* symphony. The way in which the music sinks from a C sharp major chord by a semitone (bars 14–15) certainly recalls the former, and the harmonies in this passage are more advanced than in the companion songs:

Ex. 61

Runeberg's poem, which tells of the seduction of a youth by a water-sprite who changes into many shapes before he succeeds by assuming the form of a young horse, has something of the mood of Finnish mythology about it. Though the song is by no means wholly successful it is undeniably powerful.

Till Frigga (*To Frigga*), a love song, offers another instance of an ineffective piano accompaniment using a highly restricted range of devices and those largely concentrated in the lower reaches of the keyboard. Yet in a curious way this very limitation is turned to advantage; apart from excessive length and a weak *salon*-like climax towards the end, this is a haunting song whose dark sombre hues and restrained feeling ring true. There is a moment of great poetry at the words 'Säg, hvar fostrades du, leende ängel, säg!' ('Where do you come from, smiling angel?') when the accompaniment lends an almost luminous quality to the vocal line. The voice moves stepwise most of the time; it is as if the lover were shy and inarticulate, frightened to give his ardour full rein (the line anticipates the second symphony at one point). *Drömmen* (*The Dream*), its immediate predecessor in the set, is a more conventional song: neither the semiquaver flow of the accompaniment nor the line itself is particularly distinguished, but the song is redeemed by the short middle section where the poet describes his dream. Here the contrast between dream and reality is underlined by the remoteness of the new key, F sharp minor, from the tonic F minor as well as by the interruption of the accompaniment by a wholly different piano texture. *Jägargossen* (*The young huntsman*) is an attractive song, though it has not as much personality as *Till Frigga* or *Under strandens granar*. Neither it nor the remaining two of the Op. 13 set,

Kyssens hopp (*The kiss's hope*) and *Hjärtats morgon* (*The heart's morning*), possess the more individual profile of the others.

The Op. 17 set is much finer and contains four quite masterly songs. It again consists of seven songs, whose dates range from the same period as Op. 13 (1891–2) to the very end of the decade to which *Illalle (To Evening)* and *Lastu lainehilla* (*Driftwood*) belong. This set includes *Se'n har jag ej frågat mera* (*Since then I have questioned no further*), to one of Runeberg's most famous poems, three songs to words of Tavaststjerna, and also the two above-mentioned Finnish songs. *Se'n har jag ej frågat mera* is often dated 1899, but it was in actual fact written five years earlier.[1] This must be accounted among Sibelius's most impressive and moving songs. Although it looks comparatively innocuous on paper, in performance (and more particularly in the composer's orchestral arrangement made in 1903) its eloquence and power are striking. The melodic line is drawn with firm but simple strokes, the sense of atmosphere is far more highly charged than in the earlier Runeberg settings, and the song strikes a deeper vein of feeling than anything he had done up to this time. It looks forward to an equally poignant and expressive Runeberg setting from the better-known Op. 36, *Men min fågel märks dock icke* (*But my bird is long in homing*). The three Tavaststjerna settings are a good deal slighter. *Sov in!* (*Sleep on!*) is a gentle lullaby; its successor, *Fågellek* (*Enticement*) is no less touching; indeed the simple alternation of *pianissimo* chords played in the treble effectively highlights the pathos of the vocal line. It is true to say that the melodic line in the majority of the Op. 17 songs shows a considerable advance over the preceding set: the line is much stronger and yet more supple, while the song-form as a whole seems a much more robust vehicle for the expressive demands which Sibelius makes. *Fågellek* is let down by the less inspired middle section, but it has a disarming simplicity of means.

Vilse (*Astray*) is an extraordinarily compact song whose delightful rusticity and good humour make an admirable contrast with the

[1] Alfhild Forslin, in her book *Runeberg i Musiken* (Åbo, 1958), quotes the evidence of the singer, Ida Ekman, who sang the song at a small reception at Hanslick's house in Vienna during 1895. Brahms, who was present, was a great admirer of Runeberg and warmly praised Sibelius's song.

delicate *Fågellek*. The accompaniment is astonishingly simple, but for once wholly successful: the song is over before the ear has tired of the accompanimental figure. This is not quite the case with *Illalle*, one of Sibelius's few Finnish songs, where, despite the brevity of the song, the accompanimental device is exhausted. *Illalle* (*To Evening*), sometimes known in its Swedish translation, *Om kvällen*, is justly famous: it is finer than *Vilse* because of the purity and strength of its superlative melodic line. In this song and its companion piece, *Lastu lainehilla* (*Driftwood*), Sibelius's achievement is comparable with that of Nielsen in his finest songs. There is complete harmony of means and ends. It is, incidentally, interesting that *Illalle*, *Lastu lainehilla*, and another song in Finnish written at about this time, *Souda, souda, sinisorsa* (*Swim, duck, swim!*), have some affinity. The melodic character of each song is not dissimilar, the accompaniments are confined to the simplest filling-in of harmonies, and the setting of the language is extremely supple.

It needs no special knowledge of the language to see that Sibelius alters his approach to the voice when setting Finnish. The vocal line seems to carry much of the music of the language itself: to hear this song given in Swedish is quite a different experience. Finnish is a highly inflected language, rich in vowel sounds, and these miniatures reflect Sibelius's growing confidence in handling it. On a larger scale he seems to handle Swedish more naturally, but later on in *Luonnotar* the actual sounds of the language and the vocal line are inseparable, and attempts to sing it in translation reduce its character and impact. The remaining song in Op. 17 is a Swedish setting, *En slända* (*A dragon-fly*), a fine song that anticipates the big orchestral songs like *Jubal*, although the recitative has not the boldness encountered in the latter.

Before we come to *Jubal* there is *Koskenlaski an morsiamet* (*The Ferryman's Brides*—or, to be more exact, *The Rapids-shooter's Brides*), the first of the two extended orchestral songs, the second of which is the tone-poem, *Luonnotar*. Neither in the boldness of the vocal writing nor in the musical inspiration itself does this work offer any real hint of what is to come in *Luonnotar*. Oksanen's ballad tells the story of Vilho, who takes his bride to watch him shoot the rapids at Pyörtäjä. The river-nymph, Vellamo, who cherishes a jealous passion for him, is driven to fury by the sight of his new bride and dashes a rock into the middle of the stream, thus drowning the pair. The poem ends by describing how the nymph sits mourning her love by the side of the very rock that destroyed him. Whereas in *Luonnotar* one wonders at the almost miraculous fusion of the words and the vocal line, *The Ferryman's Brides* gives little hint of this plasticity. Its idiom, not unnaturally considering its date, does not go beyond the national-romanticism we find from *Karelia* and *En Saga* down to the first symphony; and the vocal line does not differ very much from the setting of Finnish that one finds in *Kullervo* on the one hand or *The Origin of Fire* written a decade later. Certainly there is little more flexibility than in either of these: Sibelius at this time seems rather more at home when dealing with Swedish texts. Admittedly *Souda, souda, sinisorsa* might be cited to the contrary, but this is a song of very modest dimension. Musically there are fine things in *The Ferryman's Brides* (notably the poetic passage at fig. E), but for the most part it does not show the composer at his most inspired.

Although *Jubal* is the next in order of publication, ten years separate it from *The Ferryman's Brides*: all the famous songs of Opp. 36, 37, and 38 precede it. It is worth looking at the freedom and mastery with which Sibelius handles the voice, which ranges over a compass of almost two octaves. Indeed, so intense is this writing and so full of dramatic fire that one wonders whether he would not have been an opera composer of considerable note had his inclinations not carried him so far in the direction of symphonic concentration. The opening of *Jubal*, which tells how the hero sees a swan flying and swiftly draws his bow to shoot it, is a good instance of this dramatic power. Nothing could be further from the miniaturist we found in *Vilse* and the two Finnish songs of Op. 17:

Ex. 62

Its highly charged companion-piece, *Teodora*, offers yet another instance of Sibelius achieving the most complex atmosphere by the simplest of means: a seven-note figure played *pianissimo* provides the only accompaniment for three pages.

With the Op. 36 set we come to Sibelius's most popular group of songs. Despite the later opus number they precede *Jubal* and *Teodora* by almost a decade, and were written at about the same time as the first symphony. *Svarta Rosor* (*Black Roses*) is probably Sibelius's best-known song: its fascination undoubtedly lies in the darkening of the mood on the words 'ty sorgen har nattsvarta rosor' ('for sorrow has black-petalled roses'). This phrase is poised dramatically on the second inversion of the chord of C sharp minor before resolving on the C major tonic. Although it is a fine song, it pales in comparison with the second of the group, *Men min fågel märks dock icke* (*But my bird is long in homing*), to words of Runeberg. This has a simplicity of utterance, an immediately evocative atmosphere and a sheer melodic sweep that disarm criticism. Once again it is Runeberg's nature lyricism that seems to strike the deepest vein of inspiration in Sibelius. Not only is *Men min fågel märks dock icke* one of his most perfect songs, but it also ranks as one of the finest songs in the whole Scandinavian repertory. *Bollspelet vid Trianon* (*Tennis at Trianon*), to words of Fröding, is much less intense, and its charm and lightness of touch contrast well with its predecessor. The accompaniment has a delightful dance-like character, though the middle section and the very end itself strike a more sombre note. *Säf, säf, susa* (*Sigh, sedges, sigh*), sometimes known in English as *Ingalill*, thoroughly deserves its popularity. The words of Fröding's poem are extremely beautiful, and Sibelius heightens the music in them by a gentle, sighing accompaniment of a harp-like character; the return to this figure after the middle section is magical, and it is only the somewhat square climax that lowers the level of inspiration. Apart from this blemish, however, this is a fine song. So is the elegantly wrought *Marssnön* (*March snow*), though it has been somewhat overshadowed by the better-known *Demanten på marssnön* (*The Diamond on the March snow*), which for all its lyrical appeal belongs to the more conventional among Sibelius's songs.

The Op. 37 set is generally speaking less successful than either Op. 36 or Op. 38. Certainly *Den första kyssen* (*The first kiss*) fails to live up to the promise of the opening. Although the vocal line has a certain robustness, the unabashed self-indulgent romanticism of the music seems to spring more from the stock *salon* responses of late nineteenth-century song than it does from a genuinely felt experience. *Den första kyssen* seems to lack the inner vitality and freshness to survive transplanting outside its period. Sibelius's treatment of the words at the very end of the song, 'blott döden vänder ögat bort och gråter' ('only death turns aside to weep'), is redolent of Wagner. The magnetism of Wagner is far more strongly felt in *Höstkväll*. The next song of the group, *Lasse liten!* (*Little Lasse!*), is a charming lullaby with a steady haunting melodic line. Only the somewhat faltering accompaniment, which rarely strays above middle C, diminishes the effect of this song. Although its accompaniment is by no means as restricted in compass, much the same verdict can be returned on *Soluppgången* (*Sunrise*). Fortunately in none of the finest songs of Op. 36 did Sibelius's piano writing stand in his way. On the contrary, its very simplicity in *Men min fågel märks dock icke* and *Säf, säf, susa* matches the quality of the inspiration of the song as a whole. Even the next of the set, *Var det en dröm?* (*Was it a dream?*), carries an unimaginative and cumbersome piano accompaniment. But, apart from some delicacy of feeling in the transition between the second and third verses of Wecksell's poem, this is *salon* stuff and cannot be numbered among Sibelius's better songs. Nor for that matter can the inordinately popular *Flickan kom ifrån sin älsklings möte* (*The maiden came from her lover's tryst*), which shares more with the D flat major Romance for piano than just its key. It is true that the words of Runeberg's poem do not survive translation: what appears to be hack-work melodrama in English has in fact a restrained yet compelling ballad-like quality in the original Swedish. For all its lusty tunefulness and undoubted *panache* this is unworthy of the composer of *Men min fågel* or the *Arioso*, not to speak of the masterly *Höstkväll*.

Placing them side by side, one would hardly guess that the songs of Op. 37 and *Höstkväll* (*Autumn evening*) and *På verandan vid havet* (*On a balcony by the sea*) are by the same composer. Admittedly there are many individual fingerprints in *Den första kyssen*, but at no time do we glimpse the real Sibelius, the composer whose intensity of vision and spiritual stature are familiar from the great orchestral works. *Höstkväll*, on the other hand, comes from a totally different world: here is the grim, uncompromising nature poet at the height of his powers. *Höstkväll* is an astonishingly forward-looking song. Dating from 1903, the year of the first version of the violin concerto, its powerfully evoked atmosphere and magnificent sweep anticipate the world of *The Bard* and *Luonnotar*. The scoring gives some idea of the sombre colours: two oboes (no flutes), two clarinets, one bass clarinet, two bassoons, one double bassoon, four horns, three trombones, side-drum, harp and strings. Viktor Rydberg's poem seems singularly appropriate as a vehicle for Sibelius's own sympathies:

> The sun is setting, and the clouds are wandering mournfully across the sky low over the windswept lake while murmuring forests grow dusky.... Alone in desolate nature among the rocks and spindrift, a wanderer stands transfixed, rapt and exultant. He feels his soul at one with the song of the wind in the starless night. Does his sorrow die like a cry lost in the autumn's mighty lament?

The song is in the unusual key of D sharp minor and the accompaniment is largely confined to the sketchiest harmonic support, dark sustained chords and pedals. Yet for all its economy this is extremely powerful, though its effect on the piano is greatly diminished. The vocal line has the wide-ranging compass and sense of freedom that we noticed in *Jubal*; though there is a trace of Wagner at times, the whole atmosphere of the song could hardly be more individual. The setting of the words 'falken dväljes i klyftans skygd' ('the falcon sits in the shelter of a crag') up to fig. 3 in the score is unmistakably Nordic, and its lineage seems to point to *Arioso*. Here is an example of the sheer sweep of the line: note Sibelius's word-painting, and the use of the side-drum (as in *Lemminkäinen in Tuonela*) to colour the string *tremolando* pedal:

Ex. 63

This is as self-revealing a song in terms of a basic human attitude as is Ravel's *L'Indifférent.* It is no accident that the loneliness of a stranger exalted by the mystery of nature and glorying in its power should strike a sympathetic chord in Sibelius's imagination. His own art suggests a greater involvement in nature and identification with it than it does a concern with the human predicament, even though the longing for human contact is often apparent.

If *Höstkväll* has the scope if not the dramatic power of an operatic *scena*, *På verandan vid havet* (*On a balcony by the sea*), is a good deal less ambitious in scale though it is every bit as intense in feeling. The poem is also by Rydberg, and its brooding questionings are matched by the searching chromaticism of the music:

Ex. 64

The melodic line has much the same boldness as that of *Höstkväll*; since this is a much shorter song, however, the voice never takes flight so freely as it does in the earlier song. In the orchestral version the low menacing chords offer an oblique reminder of Wagner, but the whole mood and character of the song are profoundly Sibelian. The remaining three songs of this group do not maintain this high level of inspiration, though the melodic line of *I natten* (*In the night*) has a good deal of strength. Astra Desmond puts it very well when she calls it 'remarkable as a study in silence and darkness';[1] for the accompaniment is for the most part spare and terse in utterance. *Harpolekaren och hans son* (*The harper and his son*), like the preceding three songs, is to words of Rydberg; but the vocal line for all its simplicity of appeal is square and lacking in the sense of movement that characterize the finest

[1] In Gerald Abraham's symposium (pages 108–36), to which the reader is referred for a more thorough and detailed account of each song than there is space for in this volume.

songs; while in comparison with the last of the group, a setting of Fröding's *Jag ville vore i Indialand* (*I would I were in India*), it is unresourceful, being largely confined to arpeggiated chords. But neither song, *Harpolekaren* or the Fröding setting, is distinguished.

There are no songs after Op. 38 that are of comparable stature to *Höstkväll* and *På veranden vid havet*, even though there are some fine if sadly neglected miniatures. The next set in order of publication is the six songs to German texts which date from 1906. German was undoubtedly Sibelius's first foreign language, and the impulse to turn to German poets sprang in some measure from his anxiety to secure a wider degree of recognition abroad. Although many Scandinavian singers are world famous, a good many more singers of international standing have German as a mother tongue or a second language than have Swedish. Certainly the Op. 50 set have many characteristic touches and contain two very fine songs, though if must be admitted that there is none of the freedom that astonishes us in *Höstkväll*. One of the finest of the group is the third, *Im Feld ein Mädchen* (*In the field a maid sings*), whose melody is affecting and colouring sombre. The phrase-lengths of the vocal part are much more symmetrical and the line itself tends to move in stepwise manner and primary leaps. Much the same is true of its neighbour, *Aus banger brust* (*Oh, wert thou here*), which has much the same atmosphere about it as some of the incidental music to *Pelléas*. Although the piano writing is confined exclusively to a semiquaver pattern, the somewhat inconclusive ending of the song is haunting. *Sehnsucht* (*Longing*) is, like so many of his songs, handicapped by a cumbersome accompaniment which is centred far too much in the lower reaches of the piano. In *Rosalied* (*Song of the roses*), oddly enough, it is the vocal part that is vulnerable; it has a distinctly instrumental character which at one point even reminds one of the *Humoresques* for violin and orchestra. Apart from *Im Feld ein Mädchen* this set yields one quite outstanding song, *Die stille Stadt* (*The silent city*), which has an individual sense of atmosphere, a serenity and detachment and a beauty of line that mark it out from the others. This is an underrated song of great distinction and refinement of feeling which exhibits subtle shifts of harmonic emphasis. It is worthy to rank alongside some of the best of the smaller-scale Swedish settings, and has far stronger claims on the repertory than songs like *Demanten på marssnön* or *Flickan kom ifrån sin älsklings möte*.

The Josephson settings, Op. 57, and the two songs from *Twelfth Night*, Op. 60, both date from 1909, i.e. two years after the composition of *Jubal* and *Teodora*. On the whole the Josephson settings cannot be numbered among the finest Sibelius, although they contain some felicitous touches. Like the German settings they are modest in range, though none of them approaches the eloquence of *Die stille Stadt*. Undoubtedly the most powerful of them, *Jag är ett träd* (*The tree*), has a much bolder sense of line than its companions; it even offers a pallid reminder of the great songs, and the insistence of the simple chordal accompaniment is a stroke of considerable dramatic skill. The piano writing in *Näcken* (*The water-sprite*) is more enterprising than effective, but this is nevertheless one of the more interesting of the Josephson settings. *En blomma stod vid vägen* (*A flower stood by the wayside*) is a charming miniature with a simple folk-like line and a welcome example of canonic imitation between the voice and the left hand. *Kvarnhjulet* is an example of the other extreme in this group, the vocal line itself being fairly weak and the piano accompaniment no less mechanical. Nor has *Hertig Magnus* (*Duke Magnus*) much character to commend it.

The two Shakespeare songs, *Kom nu hit, död!* (*Come away, Death!*) and *Och när som jag var en smådräng* (*When that I was and a little tiny boy*), are an altogether different proposition. *Come away, Death!* is one of his greatest songs: it has intensity of vision and communicates a brooding power perfectly contained within the boundaries of the form. In the very last year of his life the composer scored this for strings and harp, but for once it is the spare monochrome of the original (for guitar or piano) that strikes home. The guitar which accompanies the singer in stage performance is the more telling, for it evokes an even sterner atmosphere. The setting is of Boruttau's Swedish translation: with some adjustment the music can be made to fit Shakespeare's own words after a fashion, though the fact remains that Sibelius's feeling for the music of the Swedish language is such that the song definitely loses something of its unity of feeling in English. Sibelius's line is sensitive to every shade of Boruttau's text; the vowel sounds, the speech inflexion and rhythm are different from the English, and as a result the song has an undeniably alien flavour when given in English. This is even more true of its delightful companion, *When that I was and a little tiny boy*, which sounds highly comic in English because of the numerous false stresses that arise. Sibelius's melody fits the rhythm and inflexion of the Swedish text like a glove.

With Op. 61 Sibelius returns to his native Finno-Swedish poets. Five of the songs, including the finest, are settings of Tavaststjerna, and the very first of the set, *Långsamt som kvällskyn* (*Slowly as the evening sun*), is in many ways the most impressive. This song is an intense mood painting which has all the concentration of atmosphere and richness of allusion that one finds in the greatest of Kilpinen's songs: it is perhaps less highly personal and less immediately attractive than *Se'n har jag ej frågat mera*, *Men min fågel märks dock icke* or the Op. 38 songs, but it is certainly as tightly packed. Without doubt this is the outstanding song of Op. 61; none of the others can match the quality of inspiration and its sense of controlled passion. Of the others the most interesting is *Romeo*, again to words by Tavaststjerna, which has greater tonal enterprise than many of the others and a more vivid and inventive accompaniment. *Vårtagen* (*Spring spell*) would be far more effective were there greater rhythmic variety in both the voice and piano part. Although they are vulnerable in other ways, the former on account of its length, *När jag drömmer* (*When I dream*) and the attractive setting of Runeberg's *Fåfäng önskan* (*Idle wishes*) are both worth a place in the repertory. However, none of these can be said to extend Sibelius's personality as a song composer in the way that *Långsamt som kvällskyn* does.

The remaining groups of songs to which Sibelius assigned opus numbers come from the war years, with the solitary exception of Op. 72, No. 6, a setting of Runeberg's *Hundra vägar* (*A hundred ways*), which dates from 1907. This has a melody of considerable flexibility and suppleness, and the alternation of various time signatures—5/2, 4/2, 3/2—matches the metrical pattern of Runeberg's poem. The modal flavouring of the harmonies as well as the texture of the piano writing occasionally lends this song the quality of a quasi-Renaissance ballad. Otherwise Op. 72 is a fairly uneven set. *Der Wanderer und der*

Bach, for instance, is altogether commonplace in spite of a comparatively effective piano part. Here it is the vocal line that suffers from rhythmic predictability and squareness. Far more interesting is *Kaiutar* (*The echo-nymph*), whose melodic line is beautifully tailored to meet the Finnish text (the very opening words are an instance in point, and their gentle fall and rise are sensitively matched in Sibelius's line). Despite the banality of the accompaniment at the beginning of this song, *Kaiutar* offers episodes that show an imaginative response to the poem. *Kyssen* (*The kiss*) is a touching song with an attractive melody: its chief limitation lies in the accompaniment, which lacks resource and variety.

Not all of the remaining songs are readily available outside the Scandinavian countries and they appear on recital programmes even more rarely than do the more famous songs. Of the Tavaststjerna settings in Op. 86, *Vår förnimmelser* (*The coming of Spring*) is a virile piece, but it is the second of the two that is the more imaginative. This is a setting of *Och finns det en tanke?* (*And is there a thought?*), a beautifully wrought miniature of the utmost simplicity. Indeed, the accompaniment consists almost exclusively of a gently undulating succession of sixths in the left hand with an occasional cry from the right. It is a poetic and touching little song.

On the whole it is true to say that none of the war-time songs after *Långsamt som kvällskyn* rank with Sibelius's best essays in the medium. Hearing the first of the Op. 88 set, *Blåsippan* (*The Anemone*), one would be tempted to date it much earlier: it is a rather sickly piece, not at all characteristic of him. Of the last set, Op. 90, again inspired by Runeberg's poetry, only the first, *Norden* (*The North*), and *Vem styrde hit din väg?* (*Who has brought you here?*), show him at somewhere near himself. There are a number of other songs to which Sibelius gave no opus number which are well worth investigating. *Souda, souda, sinisorsa* is the most famous of these; the noble *Hymn to Thais* written the year after, in 1900, shows considerable freedom in the setting of the words and hints at his handling of Swedish in the songs published during the early years of the century. Of the later songs, the fine setting of Gripenberg's *Narcissen*, written at the end of the First World War, is another that shows him in a more favourable light than some of the

Op. 86 or 88 set. If it betrays some of the limitations of range of Sibelius's songs, it has a haunting quality, a beautifully flexible and responsive handling of the Swedish language and a delicate feeling for line. This is true of a good proportion of the Swedish settings. On the evidence of these and the handful of songs which can without reservation be called great, one can claim that, although Sibelius's achievement in this medium is not commensurate with his symphonic writing, it is nevertheless very considerable.

CHAPTER XIV

CHAMBER AND INSTRUMENTAL MUSIC

ALTHOUGH Sibelius was one of the greatest masters of the orchestra it was not until he was in his mid twenties that he wrote his first orchestral piece. All his earlier works (and they are numerous) were written for various chamber groups. Yet so much has the 'silence from Järvenpää' monopolized the attention of the musical public that his subsequent lack of interest in the more ambitious chamber forms has aroused comparatively little comment. After 1892, the year of the *Kullervo* symphony, Sibelius wrote only one string quartet, a sonatina for violin and piano, along with a handful of insignificant miniatures for the same combination, whereas before that we know (or know of) some twenty or more youthful works that reached various stages of completion, including three string quartets and two violin sonatas.

The reason why his youthful energies were turned into chamber music is obvious enough: they were intended for his own immediate family circle and their friends. Indeed, the very composition of some of these groups leaves little doubt as to their *ad hoc* domestic origins. A quartet for the improbable combination of violin, cello, harmonium and piano is an instance in point. According to John Rosas's researches[1] the work is dedicated to Fru Betty Sucksdorff, whose husband was related to the Sibelius family. It seems likely that she played the harmonium, her husband the cello (Sibelius's brother Christian was an excellent cellist too) and the composer the violin. A number of the family were capable pianists. Apart from this kind of home-made music there was little else to be had in nineteenth-century Finland. Although there were periodic concerts, Helsinki did not possess a permanent symphony orchestra at the time Sibelius was born. The impact of regular orchestral concerts when he became a student in Helsinki (by which time Kajanus's orchestra was well

[1] *Otryckta kammarmusikverk av Jean Sibelius* (Åbo, 1961).

under way), and more particularly in Berlin and Vienna, was enormous. With the discovery in the nineties of his inborn flair for the orchestra it is not surprising that he temporarily laid chamber music aside. What is surprising, however, is the fact that to all intents and purposes he returned to chamber music on only one occasion, the composition in 1909 of *Voces intimae.*

Sibelius wrote a considerable number of pieces in his late teens; both Furuhjelm and Andersson speak of several one-movement trios. We know of a piano trio in A minor (1881–2), and Andersson believes that the material of the E minor piano quartet of the same year was later used in another. In any event, both of these, together with the D minor violin sonata or suite (1881–2), have been lost. His first string quartet to survive dates from the spring or summer of 1885, when he was still only nineteen. It is by all accounts a student work modelled on the Viennese classics. Certainly the opening idea is pure Haydn. The young Sibelius also wrote a string trio, in G minor, during the same year,[1] though this does not survive in its entirety. Rosas notes a greater independence of style in this work and quotes the distinctly Tchaikovskian opening of the third movement.[2] In the first movement there is even a hint of the *Valse lyrique*, Op. 96a, of 1920 at one point; this we find again in the otherwise uninteresting duo for violin and viola of the following year.

In 1887 Sibelius's chamber output included an *Andante cantabile* for violin and piano which shares the fate of the numerous trios he wrote in the summer of this year at Korpo. In later life the composer recalled one of these themes, and this I was able to see at Åbo. Its character does not greatly differ from the bulk of his music written before the end of the 1880's. From the next year two of his more important early works survive, the theme and variations in C sharp minor (for string quartet), though this is not complete, and the *Loviisa* trio. According to Levas, the *Loviisa* trio (a piano trio in C) was composed in the summer months while he was staying with Wegelius.

[1] Furuhjelm does not exclude the possibility of a later date for this work; nor does Rosas, but he does record the fact that two title-pages bear this date, one in Sibelius's own hand.

[2] *Op. cit.*, page 16.

It is by far the more interesting of the two: although its debts to classical models and in particular Beethoven are evident, Rosas finds evidence of a growing feeling for the medium. A fugue from another work, a quartet, survives from this time. Apart from the skill of the contrapuntal writing it is noteworthy for an extremely daring subject with a striking leap of a ninth and some syncopation.

The following year (1889) Sibelius produced a suite in A major for string trio, a five-movement work (*Prelude*; *Andante con moto*; *Menuetto*; *Air*; *Gigue*), though not all the manuscript survives. Furuhjelm discusses the work at considerable length,[1] although his assessment of the work is not wholly positive. It is only fair to say that Busoni thought highly of it. The string quartet in A minor, Sibelius's second essay in the medium, also dates from 1889 and won more undivided appreciation,[2] but all but the first violin part has been lost. The violin sonata in F major [3] is a three-movement work: the first adheres pretty strictly to sonata form while the remaining two are both rondos. Furuhjelm and Rosas both agree about its debts to the Grieg F major sonata, but there are nevertheless many prophetic touches.

The G minor piano quintet (1889–90) dates from Sibelius's period of study in Berlin: apart from a piano sonata that he began there at this time it is his major Berlin work. Like the A major suite and the *Voces intimae* quartet itself, it is in five movements (*Grave—Allegro* ; *Intermezzo*; *Andante*; *Scherzo*; *Moderato—Vivace*), and must be reckoned rather more seriously than these earlier pieces. The very opening *Grave* has a searching chromaticism in which Rosas detects an anticipation of the clarinet theme of the first symphony. The work evinces greater structural strength than any of its predecessors: there is evidence, to judge from the short *fugato* section from the *Intermezzo*, that Sibelius had gained much greater confidence and freedom in his part-writing. Formally he again adheres fairly closely to established procedures:

[1] Furuhjelm, *Jean Sibelius: Hans tondiktning och drag ur hans liv* (Borgå, 1916), pages 67–74.

[2] I quote Flodin's review on page 6.

[3] Furuhjelm, Levas and Johnson date this 1886 or 1886–7, but Rosas has established that it was written in the summer of 1889.

the first movement is in sonata form while three of the other movements are based on various types of rondo. At the first performance of two of the movements—the first and third—the quartet was led by the Norwegian composer and violinist Johan Halvorsen, and the pianist was Busoni.

The string quartet in B flat major was the first of these early works to which Sibelius felt inclined to give an opus number. The work dates from the autumn of 1890[1] and has four movements (*Allegro*; *Andante sostenuto*; *Presto*; *Allegro*). It represents a considerable step forward on the road to self-discovery; indeed contemporary critics found it bewildering. It is true that there are shorter episodes which remind one of Grieg, but the consensus of opinion seems to be that a genuine voice has begun to emerge. The main subject of the *Allegro* has a firmly triadic classical outline with a slight hint of Dvořák at the end of the phrase; but the student of Sibelius will immediately recognize this idea from the slow movement as an antecedent of *Rakastava*:

Ex. 65

In the following year we have the C major quartet for piano, two violins[2] and cello. This is a modest piece, written in Vienna, and consists of a slow introduction leading to a theme and variations. One of the motives in the second half of the introduction looks forward to the finale of the second symphony. Apart from an *Adagio* for string quartet written at about this time, we find that Sibelius's interest in chamber music slackens abruptly just as he begins to flex

[1] Most authorities, including Ringbom and Solanterä (as well as Johnson), accept Andersson's dating of the quartet as 1889. Rosas quotes a letter from Evalina Sibelius, as well as other material, which establishes the later date beyond any question.

[2] Not violin and viola, as stated in Grove.

his newly discovered orchestral muscles. There are one or two odd pieces; a rondo for viola and piano (1893) and a fantasy for cello and piano from the turn of the century, though both manuscripts are lost. Some scholars think the latter may well be the same as the Op. 20 *Malinconia* for cello and piano. Apart from this and the romance and epilogue, Op. 2, a much earlier piece for violin and piano that Sibelius subsequently revised, there is nothing until we come to *Voces intimae.*

Although there were reports at the time of the fourth symphony that he was working on two other string quartets, *Voces intimae* remains the only mature chamber work of substance that Sibelius wrote. Its voice seems less revealing and even less intimate than *The Bard*, but it is a good deal more personal than it appears on first acquaintance. Indeed, like *Nightride and Sunrise*, it is slow to reveal its secrets; its contours are gentler and its contrasts less extreme than in some of his more dramatic works. Both Gray and Ringbom mention its similarity of layout with some of the Haydn quartets, but this affects mostly superficial features and one can hardly imagine a more Sibelian movement than the first. Its concentration and sense of flow are never forced; on the contrary the music hides its compelling and muscular argument under a surface that seems wholly relaxed. Yet it is a remarkably taut piece with no spare matter. Much has been made of its modality: indeed Gray accepts the view that the Dorian mode is a distinguishing feature of Finnish folk-music.[1] The opening is pure D minor but the idea that immediately follows is Dorian in inflexion:

Ex. 66

[1] This was dealt with by Andersson in his article *Tonaliteten och det nationella i den finska folkmusiken* some fifteen years before Gray's book appeared, and in other articles where he showed this to be characteristic of Scandinavian folk-music as a whole, and not especially of Finland.

Sibelius makes particularly impressive use of the contrast between the modal and the tonal: the frank A major of the second group has a wonderfully smiling quality about it and the unforced momentum of the line itself is irresistible. Another magical touch is the way in which, almost without one realizing it, Sibelius moves from the exposition into the short development. So great is the sense of continuity that we are left unaware of this process of growth at the actual time it happens. There is almost a beatific quality about this movement: it is one of the purest utterances in this medium since Schubert. If the rest of the quartet were as fine it would rank among Sibelius's most perfect works.

The scherzo that follows is hardly less masterly: such is his alchemy that one is scarcely conscious of its close relationship with the first movement until the very closing bars, which directly quote the second group. However, the thematic substance is entirely drawn from the first movement. The middle movement is less impressive. Although there are many beautiful ideas in it, including its inspired opening, judged by the yardstick of the first movement it lacks the compelling concentration we expect. It is from this movement that the work apparently acquired its title: Ringbom tells us that the composer pencilled in the words *Voces intimae* over the three *ppp* chords of E minor at bar 21 in a copy of the score belonging to a friend. The passage immediately following this seems to look back nostalgically to first-period Sibelius. For all the relaxed rumination of this movement this kind of introspection seems worlds apart from the profound and bitter spiritual experience of the fourth symphony, begun only a year later. That they are near in time, however, might possibly be deduced from this figure:

Ex. 67

The *Allegretto ma pesante* is a fine movement possessed of a Haydn-esque honesty of utterance and sanity of outlook. Commentators have not been slow to point out the skill with which Sibelius transforms and comments on his material. The passage at bars 22–3 of the *Adagio* rears its head five bars after fig. 1, and the main theme itself is obviously a near relative of the first group of the movement:

Ex. 68

The finale strikes the epic note of the tone-poems, and in fact moves with a sense of momentum that almost reminds one of *Lemminkäinen's Return*. It is an exciting and exhilarating movement: that this or any other movement could be described in terms of 'tragic despair' beggars the imagination. Yet Harold Johnson says: '*Voces intimae* neither plays nor sounds like a string quartet. The impression produced on both players and listeners is that Sibelius wrote it with the strings of the orchestra in mind.' This is about as far from the truth as it is possible to imagine. A cursory examination of the score should leave no doubt to the meanest intelligence that the work is as idiomatic as any of the great classical quartets.

The only other substantial piece is the sonatina in E major for violin and piano, Op. 80, which, like the Op. 78 and Op. 79 pieces for the same combination, dates from 1915. This is a slight work, modest both in aim and achievement; it does, however, stand head and shoulders above the other violin and piano pieces. Sibelius's writing for the violin is never less than highly accomplished, and, as we know from the concerto and the *Humoresques*, it is often very much more than that. In the thirty or so pieces he wrote for this combination he is handicapped by his less than perfect command of the keyboard. The sonatina, however, though not ideal in this respect, is much more successful than some of his smaller pieces; the piano writing is never obtrusive, and is on the contrary often very effective in its own way.

The invention is delightfully fresh and spontaneous and there is never any doubt about the identity of the composer—witness the main theme of the first movement. The middle movement has a delicate, reticent charm.

Most of the other pieces from the Op. 2, which Sibelius revised in 1912, down to the *Three Pieces*, Op. 116, written in 1929, are well laid out for the instrument but are for the most part of little real moment. Of the Op. 78 set, the *Impromptu* and the *Rigaudon* are distinctly trivial, while the *Romance* might without injustice be described as Sibelius's *Salut d'amour*. The best of the set is the *Religioso*, a simple and dignified piece, dedicated to his brother Christian, a circumstance which might well explain the fact that Op. 78 is also available for cello and piano. The *Six Pieces,* Op. 79, are no less uneven: the second, *Tempo di menuetto*, and the soupy *Berceuse* are wholly unworthy of the composer. *Souvenir* abounds in Wieniawski-style virtuoso writing, and its main theme even offers echoes of Tchaikovsky. The *Sérénade* is a good deal more characteristic, and even gives us a glimpse of the kind of writing that distinguishes the *Humoresques*. The *Tanz-Idylle* has a certain wistfulness that is not unattractive.

The less said about Op. 81 the better: these pieces are pure *salon* music and not particularly good examples of their kind. Nor is the *Novellette* of Op. 102 much better. One heaves a sigh of relief on reaching the first of the *Danses champêtres*, which is at least recognizably Sibelian. The second, *Alla polacca*, and third are effective; indeed the latter is remarkably well written for the violin. But for the most part the remaining two, along with the feeble utterances of Opp. 115 and 116, are utterly undistinguished. Reading through these pieces is a somewhat depressing experience: one wonders how the composer of the seventh symphony and *The Bard* could lend himself to such shallow potboilers. The *Ballade*, the second of the Op. 115 set, is probably the best of the bunch; *The Bells* is typical of the empty showmanship which disfigures the others. Their neglect is hardly unaccountable.

CHAPTER XV

SIBELIUS AND THE PIANO

COMPOSERS who are not themselves pianists seem to experience difficulty in writing idiomatically for the keyboard. The greatest masters of keyboard writing have themselves been executants of considerable prowess or even virtuosity, and have developed in their early years an approach to the instrument that has become almost instinctive. Only in a few cases, such as Chopin or Medtner, does this seem to preclude the development of a comparable mastery of the orchestra. Certainly those composers who have not been brought up at the keyboard, and who think directly in terms of orchestral sound, either evince little interest in it or, if they do, show some degree of ineptitude in their handling of it. Berlioz and Mahler are good examples of the former. While it may be going too far to say that Sibelius falls into the second category, all but the fanatic would concede that he seemed unable to draw from the piano sounds that do justice to its genius or to his. Only rarely is sheer virtuosity in the handling of both media to be found in the same composer as it is in Debussy or Ravel.

It is true that Berlioz's genius for the orchestra developed even more rapidly than Sibelius's; but unlike Berlioz, whose keyboard writing is strictly confined to three pieces for harmonium and the odd accompaniment for songs (most of which he later orchestrated), Sibelius wrote for the piano at regular intervals throughout his life. Altogether his output comprises a sonata, the *Kyllikki* pieces, the three sonatinas, and over a hundred and twenty small pieces, the earliest, *Au crépuscule*, dating from 1887, and the last, Op. 114, from 1929. Yet even at his best, and with the exception only of the sonatinas and a handful of other pieces, he is never completely at ease; there are too many ingrained orchestral habits of mind to inhibit him. In his book Bengt de Törne quotes Sibelius as follows:[1]

> The orchestra is a huge and wonderful instrument that has got everything—except the pedal. You must always bear this in mind. You see, if you don't create an artificial pedal for your orchestration there will be holes in it, and some passages will sound ragged. Many composers, even great geniuses, either never discovered this or entirely forgot it—Liszt, for instance. . . .

A little later he describes the effect obtained at the piano when pressing the pedal, striking a *fortissimo* harmony and letting it die away:

> In the orchestra an analogous effect may be obtained by giving the beginning of the chord to trumpets, trombones, horns and woodwind, all *fortissimo*. A *diminuendo* follows and gradually the stronger instruments are dropped, leaving only horns and clarinets, flutes or bassoons to finish their *diminuendo* on the subtlest *pianissimo*. Thus you will achieve a thing of ideal beauty; it will be like a thought, born under a heavy sky and trying to reach purer regions.

Once a chord on the piano has been struck, however, it cannot be modified except by the pedal: it merely dies away and the pedal can only affect its length in so doing. Part of the genius of Sibelius's orchestral writing is the way in which a chord will suddenly be subdued in volume only to make a gradual *crescendo* afterwards. This he could not do on the piano. Yet many of his orchestral habits were carried over to the keyboard: his supporting texture is often concentrated in the lower half of the keyboard, roughly where the brass, horns and lower woodwind would normally operate. In addition he made little or no attempt to range over the whole of the keyboard: he never exploits the kind of effects obtainable at the extremities that Debussy and Ravel were masters of; nor did he appreciate the percussive possibilities of the instrument as Bartók did.

Sibelius's first piano work to be dignified with an opus number is the set of six *Impromptus*, Op. 5, which date from the early nineties. Even the Finnish writer Erik Tawaststjerna, the most enthusiastic

[1] *Sibelius—A close-up* (London, 1937), pages 31 and 33.

champion of Sibelius's piano music, admits that 'to his continental contemporaries these must have appeared highly amateurish'.[1] There is a certain folk-like directness of utterance about some of the pieces, particularly the third and fourth, but for the most part they are feeble and uninventive. Tawaststjerna assumes they are preliminary studies for the F major sonata, Op. 12 (1893), but it is only fair to say that the sonata, inept though much of the piano writing is, stands head and shoulders above the majority of Sibelius's early piano music both in quality of invention and the growing mastery of form it evinces. This is not to say that it can take its place alongside Sibelius's other music of this period; it is, as Eric Blom pointed out,[2] as orchestral as Grieg's early sonata, though there is probably more in Grieg that is conceived in terms of the keyboard than there is in Sibelius.

Despite its immaturity and uncertainty, there is a good deal to admire in this sonata. The first movement is in sonata form and, although most of the seams in the structure are clearly visible, there is a genuine sense of movement and often some attractive melodic invention. The key scheme of the movement is by no means conventional: it is evident that Sibelius's powers of thinking in terms of long paragraphs are developing. Most of the ideas are not particularly personal; they are born in the world of pale Scandinavian nationalism —Kjerulf, Grieg, Gade and Sjögren.

The Op. 24 set, which follows the sonata, comprises ten pieces written at various times between 1894 and 1903. The best of them are probably more personal than the sonata. The first two were for many years believed to be transcriptions from *Skogsrået,* written at about the same time. The *Impromptu* certainly betrays orchestral habits of mind and poses the question whether some of Sibelius's piano pieces did not begin life as orchestral sketches. It is certainly more characteristic than many of the later pieces, such as the third, *Caprice*, or the ninth, the hackneyed Romance in D flat, with its stale rhetoric and trite, *salon*-like tune. The most characteristic, however, in its melodic outline is the tenth, the *Barcarola*; the opening tune cries out for violins unison *sul* G (it is interesting to observe that Sibelius does not take the line

[1] *The Pianoforte Compositions of Jean Sibelius* (Helsinki, 1957), page 28.

[2] In Gerald Abraham, *Sibelius* (London, 1947), page 98.

below G for the first twenty-six bars). The eighth, too, called *Nocturne*, is highly individual. The harmonies are recognizably Sibelian, though the music evokes the sound of the strings; the left-hand melody seems designed for the cellos.

Kyllikki (1904), which most writers on Sibelius seem to regard as one of his best piano pieces, speaks much the same harmonic language as the second symphony and the violin concerto. It derives its title from the *Kalevala*. Kyllikki is one of the maidens of Saari; Lemminkäinen abducts her, loves her, and finally leaves her in order to try his hand with the better-known daughter of Pohjola. On the whole this is an unsuccessful piece with few attractions. One or two of the ideas are characteristic: the full-blooded opening melody is impressive (or would be in orchestral colours), and so is the *tranquillo* section in the third and final movement, which comes from the same stable as the trio section of the scherzo of the second symphony. However, the actual piano writing is sadly deficient in character and limited in resource.

Between *Kyllikki* and the sonatinas comes the set of ten pieces, Op. 58, dating from 1909. They are at best undistinguished, though the first, *Rêverie*, and the fifth, *Der Abend*, contain unmistakably Sibelian touches. But the three sonatinas, Op. 67, are an altogether different proposition. Written in 1912, a year after the fourth symphony, these are probably Sibelius's most convincing keyboard work. They are compact in design and economical in utterance: they eschew any attempts at the kind of 'effective' piano writing which Sibelius made in the Op. 24 set. None of the movements is very long; they average less than two minutes in duration, so that there is no time for any development along the lines familiar in the bigger works.

The first—in A major according to the title-page, though it is in fact in the relative minor, F sharp—is linear in style: the texture is much more spare than we find in *Kyllikki*; this is a feature that is common to all three sonatinas. Indeed, not only in matters of keyboard layout but also of the suitability of the ideas to the medium, this sonatina shows a considerable advance over Sibelius's earlier work. This idea, for instance, is memorably pianistic and falls conveniently under the fingers:

Ex. 69

In addition this and the other two movements are recognizably Sibelian. Not only is the texture *dépouillé* but the proportions are most skilfully balanced. Sibelius rests content with one short idea which is never developed *in extenso*. Yet despite its brevity the finale of this sonatina still retains his characteristic sense of forward movement.

The F sharp minor sonatina is the most perfect of all his piano works, but the remaining two, in E major and B flat minor respectively, are very nearly as fine. The canonic imitation in the first movement of the E major is wholly successful: there is no sense of strain, no feeling that too scholarly an apparatus is imposed on too lightweight a substance. There is an enviable harmony of means and ends in these three pieces, for the texture is always lightened to match the melodic character of the music. Though they do not look effective on paper, they come off remarkably well in performance. The third and last, in B flat minor, employs related thematic material in all its three movements. The *Andante* is the most vulnerable from the pianistic point of view, but in the hands of a sensitive player even its bare octave writing can be made to sound effective. The melody itself has vague overtones of Rimsky-Korsakov.

The sonatinas score on the grounds of their sheer economy of ideas, layout and form. When Sibelius attempts more ambitious concentrations of keyboard sonority, as in the opening bars of *The Village Church*, Op. 103, No. 1, or in the *Romance*, Op. 101, No. 1, he does not wholly succeed in banishing thoughts of the orchestra. Immediately following the sonatinas and closely related to them in character are the two *Rondinos*, Op. 68. Eric Blom's theory that these may have been intended as movements for incomplete sonatinas seems highly probable. The reflective and very beautiful G sharp minor

Rondino could well be a slow movement to an unfinished sonatina. Its expressive leaps of a minor ninth and its plastic improvisatory line are poetic and recall a vaguely Scriabinesque mood, even though the harmonic language is less complex. The *Rondino* in C sharp minor would make a delightful finale to a work of this kind.

The sonatinas and *Rondinos* were published in 1912, and can be regarded as a relaxation from the world of the fourth symphony, *The Bard* and *Luonnotar*. The next batch of pieces comes from 1914, when the war forced Sibelius into publishing sets of potboilers. Between them, the three sets, Opp. 74, 75 and 76, comprise no fewer than twenty-one miniatures. The *Four Lyric Pieces*, Op. 74, have been overshadowed by the comparatively popular Op. 75, the superiority of which is generally undisputed. The first, *När rönnen blommar* (*When the rowan blossoms*), is a delicate piece that has been compared with the first *Rondino*, though it misses its wayward poetic quality. *Den ensamma furan* (*The lonely fir*) has a genuine nobility, though it is easy to hear the weight of the unison strings in the triplet quavers in bar 10. Similarly, in the fourth piece, *Björken* (*The Birch*), the second half cries out for muted strings with perhaps the delicate rustle from the side-drum that accompanied the middle section of *Lemminkäinen in Tuonela*. The last piece, *Granen* (*The Spruce*), is far more pianistic, even though the arpeggiated writing marked *risoluto* is not wholly effective. By far the best of the set is the third, *Aspen* (*The Ash*), an eloquent piece with a feeling of resigned melancholy that is thoroughly individual and memorable.

It is difficult to share Tawaststjerna's enthusiasm for all of the Op. 76 set. None of the thirteen pieces seems as good as *The Ash*, save perhaps the magnificent *Twinflower of the North*, an original piece that at first glance looks Schumannesque on paper. Of the others, the second, *Étude*, maintains an amiable but brainless patter in the style of so much children's music. A similar study is the *Pièce enfantine*, which one would never imagine in a thousand years to be the work of Sibelius. A great many of the earlier sets, Op. 34 (1914–16) and the *Pensées lyriques*, Op. 40 (1912–14), seem equally unworthy, though there is at least one outstanding exception, the *Pensée mélodique*, Op. 40, No. 6. This is a haunting piece whose frequent modulations are as charged with melancholy as the Szymanowski *Mazurkas*, Op. 50. This piece is worthy to rank alongside the first of the *Rondinos* and deserves a place in the repertory.

The next batch of pieces, Op. 85, dates from 1916. These all bear floral titles and have considerable charm. Most delightful is *The Snapdragon*, which despite its apparently platitudinous sequences has an alluring quality that belies the notion that Sibelius lacks humour. Whatever their shortcomings these pieces are characteristic Sibelius, which is more than can be said for the later piano pieces, Op. 94 (1919), Op. 97 (1920) and Op. 99 (1922). More personal, though by no means Sibelius at his most interesting, are the two sets, Op. 101 (1923) and Op. 103 (1924). They seem far closer to the world of the *Suite mignonne* and *Suite champêtre* than they do to the sixth and seventh symphonies. *In mournful mood* (the pieces have English titles) from Op. 103 is as trivial as *The Storm*, its immediate predecessor, is ineffective. By far the most imaginative piece is the *Scène romantique*, Op. 101, No. 5, which has an atmospheric opening, even though this level of inspiration is not really maintained.

There is little doubt that Sibelius is not really at home in piano music. A comparison with the piano works of Nielsen is very much to his disadvantage. Nielsen's *Chaconne*, the *Theme and Variations*, Op. 40, the *Suite*, Op. 45, and the late Op. 59 pieces are bigger in scope and forward-looking in technique. They make use of devices and sonorities which Sibelius never attempted to employ. It is significant that a composer of his stature, who could think more organically than any of his immediate contemporaries, should have confined himself to miniatures where the keyboard was concerned. Nielsen made none of Sibelius's pianistic blunders; his writing is admirably balanced though often difficult to play. His textures are never overweighted in the bass by thick chords when the right hand is relatively light (even confined to a single line). The fact is that Sibelius's music for the piano yields a handful of miniatures that have genuine charm, as well as the three sonatinas which show evidence of real mastery. Were they, however, the only work to survive we would have no inkling of his real stature. Sibelius's evident reluctance to undertake a big work in this medium suggests his recognition of this shortcoming.

CHAPTER XVI

HIS REPUTATION AND STATURE

TASTE is never static: composers accepted as masters during their lifetime, like Telemann and Spohr, quite often recede into relative obscurity only a few years after their death. Unfortunately it is not only the second- or third-rate composer who is subject to these shifts in public interest and huddled off to comfortless neglect. Even the great masters are not exempt. At the end of the nineteenth century Bernard Shaw could write of the scandalous neglect of Mozart in London, while Mendelssohn, who reigned supreme in Victorian England, enjoyed a comparatively inferior status at the beginning of the post-war era. Bach was neglected for almost a century after his death.

Sibelius was fortunate in receiving during his lifetime veneration and fame on a scale that few other composers have enjoyed. However, as his critics are quick to point out, apart from Finland and the Scandinavian countries, his music gained a real hold over the public only in the Anglo-Saxon countries. Although he has many admirers in France, Sibelius has made comparatively little headway as far as the concert repertory is concerned. French taste is notoriously insular: Bruckner and Mahler are seldom heard there and it is only in recent years that Brahms, who for years remained relatively unplayed, has gained acceptance as a classic. This might well happen to Sibelius in time. In Germany he has won more frequent hearing but not, as yet, an unchallenged place in the permanent repertory, though he had distinguished advocacy from conductors such as Rosbaud, and Karajan and Maazel continue the tradition. Germany, so long the centre of the European symphonic tradition, is slow to accept outsiders like Sibelius, Vaughan Williams and Elgar.

As far as the French are concerned, their reluctance to accept Sibelius may be in some measure temperamental. Sibelius's is a world that is as personal as Berlioz's. Indeed the parallel with Berlioz is worth pursuing, for he too is a composer who has kindled the most profound controversy—hailed by his admirers as a great master and denounced by others no less vehemently as an amateur and a charlatan. It is, strangely enough, in Britain too that Berlioz has the most vocal and devoted following, and where he enjoys at the present time a measure of public support that is not surpassed even in his own country. Both Berlioz and Sibelius are profoundly original composers, self-forming, uncompromising and new; indeed, if originality were the sole criterion of greatness in music, Berlioz would probably be counted as the greatest master of them all. But just as Sibelius meets with little response in France, Berlioz meets with similar incomprehension in the Scandinavian countries. In both cases, perhaps, ignorance of their work has facilitated the erection of artificial barriers which might well be swept away had either composer won a sufficient hearing. But to some extent it is a matter of temperamental disaffinity: the impulsive flow of invention, the white-hot, feverish temperature, the asymmetric melodic thinking, the vivid colouring and the absence of reticence in Berlioz are elements which strike the Scandinavian sensibility as theatrical. Similarly the regional flavouring of much of Sibelius's nature poetry, identified so intimately with the northern landscape, the icy intensity of some of the inspiration (which obscures for the casual listener its profound inner warmth) and the non-episodic nature of his thinking do not win favour among French audiences, who are no more receptive to unfamiliar modes of thought than they were in the time of Berlioz.

England, however, responded warmly to Sibelius's music from the very beginning, when his work was introduced by Richter, Bantock and Henry Wood in the early years of the century. It was in the thirties that the round of Sibelius festivals, the formation of the Sibelius Society and the constant appearance of his music in concert programmes led to his recognition as a classic. That his standing would come to be questioned after his death in the fifties was inevitable in the natural course of events: the claims made by Gray that Sibelius would 'ultimately prove to have been, not only the greatest of his generation, but one of the major figures in the entire history of music' were bound to be re-examined. The climate of critical opinion in this country hardened against Sibelius during the fifties; Mahler, on the other hand, began to make greater headway. During the thirties Mahler had fewer champions among conductors and critics in England and his work was expensive to mount. After the war, when the B.B.C. Third Programme and the gramophone companies made available authentic performances of his work, he began to win a considerable public following. Delius's oft-quoted but prophetic remarks are worth recalling: 'Now, it's Sibelius, and when they're tired of him, they'll boost up Mahler and Bruckner.'

At the same time it is only proper to add that the swing against Sibelius took place in this country among a small group of critics rather than among the public, who continue to attend concerts at which his work appears and to buy his symphonies on records. Admittedly the public following is for the Sibelius of the second symphony and the violin concerto; the loftiest of his works—*Tapiola*, *Luonnotar* and the fourth and sixth symphonies—do not reach so wide an audience. For the simple-minded critic who equates the complexity of harmonic language and a higher norm of dissonance with the idea of musical 'progress' (an essentially nineteenth-century concept), Sibelius is not as great a composer as Schönberg or Bartók, simply because he was content to leave the language of music very much as he found it. He used an already existing vocabulary as Bach did, but in so highly idiosyncratic a manner that no attempt to imitate it can succeed. The self-styled 'progressive' will dismiss him much in the same way that the contemporaries of Bach tended to relegate him to the second rank because he was 'old-fashioned'. This is to confuse language and style. There are few greater masters of musical syntax than Sibelius: what is extraordinary is his capacity for making a simple chord sound his own.

Yet admirers of Sibelius must concede that, in contradistinction to Palestrina or Bach, his world has circumscribed limits and a less-than-universal appeal. Indeed it is questionable whether his range of feeling is as wide as his still underrated contemporary, Nielsen. In his weaker moments Sibelius seems the prisoner of his own highly personal mode of utterance—a fate which but rarely overtakes Nielsen, who demonstrates a much more cosmopolitan outlook without ever losing his sense of identity. Why should this be the case? To a large extent it can be explained in terms of centrality of experience. Sibelius has an acutely developed sense of identification with nature and a preoccupation with myth that at one and the same time define his unique strength and his basic limitation. These preoccupations override his involvement in the human predicament, except in so far as it affects man's relationship with nature. This is not to deny that as a nature poet he expresses feelings that can be shared by all, a sense of nature's awe and power, even though the very nature with which he is concerned is regional. There is a strong feeling for nature in Mahler, but it is not the predominant factor in his musical make-up as it is in Sibelius. What makes Sibelius's achievement the greater, in spite of Mahler's centrality of experience, his greater warmth and his dramatic awareness, is that as a symphonist he imposes a greater degree of order on the materials of the symphony and exercises a greater discipline in the selection of these very materials. Mahler, whose sense of form is not to be underrated, was still prepared to offer, as it were, the raw materials of experience as if they were in themselves a finished work of art. The compulsion they exert is that of the poignant human document that overwhelms because of the variety and intensity of its emotional climate. Sibelius's way is fundamentally more classical because he refuses to treat certain states of mind and feeling in the context of the symphony. Without wishing in any sense to belittle the achievement of other masters of this period, such as Mahler, Strauss, Elgar and Debussy, there is little doubt that none of them had the highly developed sense of form that Sibelius had. 'What distinguishes genius from talent is condensation, which is related to brevity, but not identical with it,' wrote Einstein in *Greatness in Music.*

All were masters of the orchestra. Debussy's achievement in terms of new sonorities and enrichment of language is greater than Sibelius's. His command of the media in *La Mer, Pelléas et Mélisande*, the sonata for flute, viola and harp, and the *Préludes* for piano witnesses greater virtuosity; his debt to inherited tradition was even less than Sibelius's. Debussy was capable in the *Petite Suite* of writing light music that is every bit as perfect as that of Sibelius in his *Pelléas* or *Humoresques* for violin and orchestra; but he was incapable of turning out the quantities of third-rate light music that poured from Sibelius's pen in such embarrassing profusion. Yet even in Debussy's greatest works we find a reliance on short phrase patterns that are repeated. *Nuages* is an obvious case of Debussy constructing a highly poetic mosaic of repeated two-bar phrases; rarely do we find anything remotely resembling the kind of growth that we meet in Sibelius. But so unique is his inspiration and so integrated is his musical personality that these two-bar patterns and their repetitions never disturb us as they do on occasion in the work of another noble nature poet, Janáček. On the other hand, nowhere in Debussy do we find the elevated heroic spirit of the seventh symphony.

Sibelius's capacity for what one might term 'continuous creation' in the symphonies and symphonic poems has few parallels; to find them one has to look among the composers of the very first rank. When Professor Abraham wrote of the third symphony's first movement that it was comparable only with the great classical masters, he was in no sense exaggerating. This, together with the last four symphonies, shows a feeling for form that never fails to astonish, however often one analyses them. W. G. Hill, who confessed a temperamental disaffinity for Sibelius, and investigated his art from the point of view of an uncommitted if not hostile critic, was led (albeit reluctantly) to a growing admiration for its breathtaking formal mastery.[1] Why, then, as total experiences are they not in the final resort as great as the symphonies of Beethoven or Brahms? It must be admitted that, great though he is, Sibelius does not belong to the 'super-giants' of the order of Bach, Handel, Haydn, Mozart, Beethoven and Schubert, whose numbers barely exceed a dozen. These masters record a greater wealth, range and depth of experience; theirs is an inexhaustibility of spirit, and what they say has a universality of application that seems untied to any particular time or place. It is arguable whether a master of this order has yet come to light in the present century.

While Sibelius can be said to transcend the period in a way in which a highly self-conscious figure like Stravinsky does not, he

[1] 'Some Aspects of Form in the Symphonies of Sibelius' (*Music Review*, 1949).

cannot be said to be independent of place in a way that Stravinsky is. What Sibelius has to say is intimately related to the atmosphere and sensibility of northern Europe—just as Mussorgsky is related to the Russian ethos. In that lies his strength. Sibelius does, however, respond to nature in a way that unites two traditions—that of the nineteenth-century tone-poem together with the classical tradition with its concern for tonal change and dramatic contrast. This primary concern with nature has universal application but at the same time excludes some areas of feeling. There is little sense of the transience of human experience that we find in Elgar; there is little of the innate capacity for suffering and the inborn grace and innocence that one finds in Schubert. He is rarely vulnerable in the way that Schubert is, save perhaps in *Rakastava*. Yet, among the twentieth-century masters from Debussy and Bartók to Stravinsky, the quietism of the sixth symphony or the profoundly searching *Tapiola* has no parallel. Of the half-dozen or so great composers of the present century he will not be found to be the least.

APPENDICES

APPENDIX A

CALENDAR

(Figures in brackets in last column denote the age at which the person mentioned died)

Year	*Age*	*Life*	*Contemporary Musicians*
1865		Born in Hämeenlinna, Dec. 8.	Albeniz 5; Alkan 52; Arensky 4; Auber 83; Balakirev 28; Berlioz 63; Berwald 69; Bizet 27; Boito 23; Borodin 32; Brahms 32; Bruch 27; Bruckner 41; Chabrier 24; Chausson 10; Cornelius 41; Cui 30; Dargomizhsky 52; Debussy 3; Delius 3; Dukas born, Oct. 1; Duparc 17; Dvořák 24; Elgar 8; Fauré 20; Fibich 15; Foerster 6; Franck 43; Gade 48; Glazunov born, Aug. 10; Gounod 47; Grechaninov 1; Grieg 22; Halvorsen 1; Hubay 7; Humperdinck 11; d'Indy 14; Janáček 11; Kajanus 10; Kjerulf 50; Lalo 42; Liadov 10; Liapounov 6; Liszt 54; Magnard born, June 9; Mahler 5; Martucci 9; Moniuszko 46; Mussorgsky 26; Nielsen born, June 9; Nordraak 22; Offenbach 46; Parry 17; Puccini 7; Rimsky-Korsakov 21; Rossini 73; Ropartz 1; Saint-Saëns

Year	Age	Life	Contemporary Musicians
			30; Sinding 9; Smetana 41; Söderman 33; Stanford 13; Strauss 1; Svendsen 26; Taneiev 9; Tchaikovsky 25; Thomas 57; Verdi 52; Wagner 52; Wolf 5; Ysaÿe 7.
1866	1		Busoni born, April 1; Kalinnikov born, Jan. 13; Nordraak (23) dies, March 20; Satie born, May 17.
1867	2		Granados born, July 29.
1868	3	Father's death (July 31).	Bantock born, Aug. 17; Berwald (71) dies, April 3; Kjerulf (52) dies, Aug. 11; Rossini (76) dies, Nov. 13.
1869	4		Berlioz (66) dies, March 8; Dargomizhsky (56) dies, Jan. 17; Järnefelt born, Aug. 14; Pfitzner born, May 5; Roussel born, April 5.
1870	5		Lekeu born, Jan. 20; Novák born, Dec. 5; Florent Schmitt born, Sept. 28.
1871	6		Auber (89) dies, May 12; Scriabin born, Dec. 25; Stenhammar born, Feb. 7.
1872	7		Alfvén born, May 1; Moniuszko (53) dies, June 4; Vaughan Williams born, Oct. 12.
1873	8		Rachmaninov born, March 20; Reger born, March 19.
1874	9	First regular piano lessons.	Cornelius (50) dies, Oct. 26; Holst born, Sept. 21; Ives born, Oct. 20; Franz Schmidt born, Dec. 22; Schönberg born, Sept. 13; Suk born, Jan. 4.

Appendix A—Calendar

Year	*Age*	*Life*	*Contemporary Musicians*
1875	10	First attempts at composition, including *Vattendroppar.*	Bizet (37) dies, June 3; Glière born, Jan. 11; Hahn born, Aug. 19; Ravel born, March 7.
1876	11	Entry into Hämeenlinna *Suomalainen Normaalilyseo.*	Falla born, Nov. 23; Ruggles born, March 11; Söderman (43) dies, Feb. 10.
1877	12		Dohnányi born, July 27.
1878	13		Caplet born, Nov. 23; Palmgren born, Feb. 16; Schreker born, March 23.
1879	14		Ireland born, Aug. 13; Medtner born, Dec. 24; Respighi born, July 9.
1880	15	Begins study of the violin with Gustav Levander.	Bloch born, July 20; Offenbach (61) dies, Oct. 4; Pizzetti born, Sept. 20.
1881	16	Studies Marx's *Lehre von der musikalischen Composition.*	Bartók born, March 25; Enesco born, Aug. 19; Miaskovsky born, April 20; Mussorgsky (42) dies, March 28.
1882	17	Piano trio in A minor.	Kodály born, Dec. 16; Malipiero born, March 18; Stravinsky born, June 17.
1883	18		Bax born, Nov. 6; Casella born, July 25; Szymanowski born, Sept. 21; Wagner (70) dies, Feb. 13; Webern born, Dec. 3.
1884	19	Andantino for cello and piano.	Rangström born, Nov. 30; Smetana (60) dies, May 12.
1885	20	Passes *studentexamen* (May 15) and begins law studies at Helsinki: completes string quartet in E flat.	Berg born, Feb. 7; Riegger born April 29; Varèse born Dec. 22; Wellesz born, Oct. 21.
1886	21	Abandons law studies to devote himself entirely to music.	Liszt (75) dies, July 31; Schoeck born, Sept. 1.
1887	22	Becomes second violin in	Borodin (53) dies, Feb. 20;

Appendix A—Calendar

Year	Age	Life	Contemporary Musicians
		Helsinki conservatoire's quartet.	Madetoja born, Feb. 17; Fartein Valen born, Aug. 25; Villa-Lobos born, March 5.
1888	23	*Svartsjukans nätter* composed, violin pieces, Op. 2. Friendship with Busoni (22).	Alkan (75) dies, March 29.
1889	24	Completes studies in Helsinki: suite in A major and a string quartet in A minor performed. Composes quartet, Op. 4, and wins *Kiseleffska stipendium* from *Nylandsnation*, travels to Germany (Sept. 7). Composes G minor piano quintet: meets Kajanus (34) and hears his *Aino* symphony.	Shaporin born, Nov. 8.
1890	25	Engagement to Aino Järnefelt (autumn). Performance of string quartet in B flat, Op. 4. Journey to Vienna, where he makes first attempts at orchestral composition.	Franck (68) dies, Nov. 8; Gade (73) dies, Dec. 21; Ibert born, Aug. 15; Frank Martin born, Sept. 15; Martinů born, Dec. 8; Nystroem born, Oct. 13.
1891	26	Orchestral overture completed, sketches of *Kullervo* begun: also piano quartet in C, and an octet for flute, clarinet and strings, whose material he uses in *En Saga*.	Prokofiev born, April 23.
1892	27	Successful first performance of *Kullervo* symphony (April 28); composition of *En Saga*. Marriage to Aino Järnefelt (June 10) and appointment as teacher of composition at conservatoire.	Honegger born, March 10; Yrjö Kilpinen born, Feb. 4; Lajtha born, June 30; Lalo (69) dies, April 22; Milhaud born, Sept. 4; Rosenberg born, June 6.
1893	28	*Karelia* music, *Swan of Tuonela* and piano sonata in F completed.	Goossens born, May 26; Gounod (75) dies, Oct. 18; Haba born, June 21; Tchaikovsky (53) dies, Nov. 6.

Year	*Age*	*Life*	*Contemporary Musicians*
1894	29	*Vårsång* for orchestra, *Skogsrået* (to words of Rydberg). Visits to Italy and Bayreuth.	Chabrier (53) dies, Sept. 13; Lekeu (24) dies, Jan. 21; Moeran born, Dec. 31; Pijper born, Sept. 8; Piston born, Jan. 20.
1895	30	Continues work on the *Four Legends*, Op. 22.	Hindemith born, Nov. 16.
1896	31	*Jungfrun i tornet* composed and first performed (Nov. 7).	Bruckner (72) dies, Oct. 11; Sessions born, Dec. 28; Thomas (85) dies, Feb. 12.
1897	32	Award of annual pension from Finnish Government; begins work on *King Christian* suite.	Brahms (64) dies, April 3; Cowell born, March 11; Saeverud born, April 17; Tansman born, June 12.
1898	33	Performance of *King Christian* (Feb. 24). Visit to Berlin.	Roy Harris born, Feb. 12.
1899	34	*Atenarnas sång, Scènes historiques* I, and first symphony (perf. April 26). *Finlandia* and the songs, Op. 36, composed.	Chausson (44) dies, June 10; Chávez born, June 13; Poulenc born, Jan. 7; Revueltas born, Dec. 31.
1900	35	S. visits Paris during tour with Helsinki Orchestra (July–Aug).	Burkhard born, April. 17; Copland born, Nov. 14; Fibich (49) dies, Oct. 15. Klami born, Sept. 20; Křenek born, Aug. 23.
1901	36	S. visits Rapallo (Feb.) and Prague, where he meets Dvořák (60) and Suk (27); conducts his own music in Germany. He revises *En Saga* and begins second symphony. Relinquishes teaching post at Helsinki.	Kalinnikov (34) dies, Jan. 11; Rubbra born, May 23; Verdi (87) dies, Jan. 27.
1902	37	Second symphony performed (March 8).	Shebalin born, June 11; Walton born, March 29.
1903	38	Completes original version of violin concerto (summer) and *Romance* in C for strings.	Berkeley born, May 12; Blacher born, Jan. 3; Wolf dies, Feb. 22.

Year	*Age*	*Life*	*Contemporary Musicians*
1904	39	Moves to Järvenpää and begins third symphony (Sept.). Songs, Op. 38, including *Höstkväll* and *På verandan vid havet*; *Kyllikki* for piano.	Dallapiccola born, Feb. 3; Dvořák (63) dies, May 1; Kabalevsky born, Dec. 30; Petrassi born, July 16.
1905	40	Conducts second symphony in Berlin (Jan.). Composes music to *Pelléas et Mélisande* (spring). Revised version of violin concerto first perf. with Strauss conducting (Oct.). First visit to England.	Hartman born, Aug. 2; Lambert born, Aug. 23; Seiber born, May 4; Tippett born, Jan. 2; Dag Wirén born, Oct. 15.
1906	41	Composes *Belshazzar's Feast* and *Pohjola's Daughter*.	Arensky (44) dies, Feb. 25; Shostakovich born Sept. 25.
1907	42	Completes third symphony (perf. Sept. 25); Mahler visits Helsinki (Nov.).	Grieg (64) dies, Sept. 4.
1908	43	Second visit to England, where he conducts third symphony at R.P.O. concert (Feb. 20). Composes music to *Swanwhite* at Järvenpää. Operation in Helsinki (May) and visit to Berlin. Begins *Voces intimae*.	Rimsky-Korsakov (64) dies, June 21; Messaien born, Dec. 10; Larsson born, May 15.
1909	44	Completes *Voces intimae* in London. Songs, Op. 57, and *In Memoriam* composed.	Albeniz (48) dies. May 18; Holmboe born, Dec. 20; Martucci (53) dies, June 1.
1910	45	Begins fourth symphony and composes songs, Op. 61.	Balakirev (73) dies, May 29; Barber born, March 9; William Schuman born, Aug. 4.
1911	46	Concert tour in Sweden and the Baltic States (Feb.). Completion and first perf. of fourth symphony (April 3). Visit to Berlin (Oct.) and Paris (Nov.), where he hears much new music. *Rakastava* for strings and percussion completed.	Mahler (50) dies, May 29 Svendsen (70) dies, June 14.

Year	*Age*	*Life*	*Contemporary Musicians*
1912	47	S. invited to become professor at Vienna. Second series of *Scènes historiques*, three sonatinas for piano. Visit to London, where he conducts fourth symphony.	
1913	48	*The Bard* and *Luonnotar* composed.	Britten born, Nov. 22.
1914	49	Visit to America (May) where he receives honorary degree at Yale; composes *The Oceanides* and begins sketching the fifth symphony.	Liadov (59) dies, Aug. 28; Magnard (49) dies, Sept. 3.
1915	50	First version of fifth symphony completed; sonatina for violin and piano, Op. 80, settings of Fröding, Op. 84; concert tour in Scandinavia.	Scriabin (43) dies, April 27; Taneiev (58) dies, Jan. 19.
1916	51	Revised version of fifth symphony performed (Dec.).	Ginastera born, April 11; Granados (48) dies, March 24; Reger (42) dies, May 11.
1917	52	Runeberg songs, Op. 90.	
1918	53	Finnish civil war. Järvenpää searched by Red troops (Feb.). S. moves to Helsinki (March).	Boito (76) dies, June 10; Cui (83) dies, March 24; Debussy (55) dies, March 25; Parry (70) dies, Oct. 7.
1919	54	Definitive version of fifth symphony (autumn).	Niels Viggo Bentzon born, Aug. 24.
1920	55	*Maan virsi*, Op. 95, orchestral pieces, Op. 96, *Six Bagatelles* for piano, Op. 97. Invited to become head of the Eastman School of Music.	Bruch (82) dies, Oct. 2; Fricker born, Sept. 5.
1921	56	Last visit to London (Jan.), where he is reunited with Busoni (55). Composes *Suite mignonne* and *Suite champêtre*.	Humperdinck (67) dies, Sept. 27; Saint-Saëns (86) dies Dec. 16.
1922	57	*Suite caractéristique* for orchestra and piano pieces, Op. 99.	Lukas Foss born, Aug. 15.

Year	Age	Life	Contemporary Musicians
1923	58	Concert tour of Norway and Sweden (Jan.); conducts first perf. of sixth symphony (Feb. 19). Visit to Rome, where he conducts at the Augusteo (March 11).	Peter Mennin born, May 17.
1924	59	Completes seventh symphony (March).	Busoni (58) dies, July 27; Fauré (79) dies, Nov. 4; Liapounov (64) dies, Nov. 8; Puccini (65) dies, Nov. 29; Stanford (71) dies, March 29.
1925	60	*Tapiola.*	Caplet (46) dies, April 22; Satie (59) dies, July 1.
1926	61	Incidental Music to *The Tempest* written for production in Copenhagen.	Boulez born, March 23; Henze born, July 1.
1927	62		Stenhammar (56) dies, Nov. 20.
1928	63		Janáček (74) dies, Aug. 12.
1929	64	Last published work with opus no.: *Three Pieces* for violin and piano, Op. 116. Enters into retirement at Järvenpää.	
1930	65		
1931	66		d'Indy (80) dies, Dec. 2; Nielsen (66) dies, Oct. 2; Ysaÿe (73) dies, May 12.
1932	67		
1933	68		Duparc (85) dies, Feb. 13; Kajanus (78) dies, July 6.
1934	69		Delius (72) dies, June 10; Elgar (77) dies, Feb. 23; Holst (60) dies, May 25; Schreker (55) dies, March 21.
1935	70		Berg (50) dies, Dec. 24; Dukas (69) dies, May 18; Halvorsen (71) dies, Dec. 4; Suk (61) dies, May 29.

Appendix A—Calendar

Year	*Age*	*Life*	*Contemporary Musicians*
1936	71		Glazunov (70) dies, March 21; Respighi (56) dies, April 18.
1937	72		Ravel (62) dies, Dec. 28; Roussel (68) dies, Aug. 23; Szymanowski (54) dies, March 29.
1938	73		
1939	74		Franz Schmidt (64) dies, Feb. 11.
1940	75		Revueltas (40) dies, Oct. 5.
1941	76		Sinding dies (85), Dec. 3.
1942	77		
1943	78		Rachmaninov (69) dies, March 28.
1944	79		
1945	80		Bartók (64) dies, Sept. 26; Webern (61) dies, Sept. 15.
1946	81		Bantock (78) dies, Oct. 16; Falla (69) dies, Nov. 14.
1947	82		Casella (63) dies, May 15; Hahn (71) dies, Jan. 28; Madetoja (60) dies, Oct. 6; Pijper (52) dies, March 19; Rangström (62) dies, May 11.
1948	83		
1949	84		Novák (78) dies, July 18; Pfitzner (80) dies, May 22; Strauss (85) dies, Sept. 8.
1950	85		Miaskovsky (69) dies, Aug; Moeran (55) dies, Dec. 1.
1951	86		Foerster (91) dies, May 29; Lambert (45) dies, Aug. 21; Medtner (71) dies, Nov. 13; Palmgren (73) dies, Dec. 13; Schönberg (76) dies, July 13.
1952	87		Fartein Valen (65) dies, Dec. 14.
1953	88		Bax (69) dies, Oct. 3; Prokofiev (61) dies, March 4.

Year	*Age*	*Life*	*Contemporary Musicians*
1954	89		Ives (80) dies, May 19.
1955	90		Burkhard (55) dies, June 18; Enesco (74) dies, May 14; Honegger (63) dies, Nov. 27; Ropartz (91) dies, Nov. 22.
1956	91		Glière (81) dies, June 23; Grechaninov (91) dies, Jan. 5.
1957	91	Sibelius dies of a cerebral haemorrhage in Järvenpää (Sept. 20).	Alfvén 85, Barber 47, Niels Viggo Bentzon 38; Berkeley 54, Blacher 54, Bloch 77, Boulez 32, Britten 44, Chavez 58, Copland 57, Cowell 60, Dallapiccola 53, Dohnányi 80, Foss 35, Fricker 37, Ginastera 41, Goossens 64, Haba 64, Roy Harris 59, Hartman 52, Henze 32, Hindemith 62, Holmboe 48, Ibert 67, Ireland 78, Järnefelt 88, Kabalevsky 52, Yrjö Kilpinen 65, Klami 57, Kodály 75, Křenek 57, Lajtha 65, Larsson 49, Malipiero 75, Martin 67, Martinů 67, Mennin 34, Milhaud 65, Nystroem 65, Petrassi 53, Piston 63, Pizzetti 77, Poulenc 58, Riegger 72, Rosenberg 65, Rubbra 56, Ruggles 81, Saeverud 60, Schmitt 87, Schoeck (81) dies, Schumann 47, Seiber 52, Sessions 61, Shaporin 68, Shebalin 55, Shostakovich 51, Stravinsky 75, Tansman 60, Tippett 52, Varèse 72, Vaughan Williams 85, Villa Lobos 70, Walton 55, Wellesz 72, Dag Wirén 52.

APPENDIX B

CATALOGUE OF WORKS

Orchestral Works

Op.		*Date*
6.	*Cassazione*. Two pieces. MS.	1904
9.	*En Saga*.	1892, 1901
10.	*Karelia* Overture.	1893
11.	*Karelia* Suite.	1893
	1. Intermezzo	
	2. Ballade	
	3. Alla marcia	
14.	*Rakastava* (The Lover). For strings and percussion.	1911
	1. The Lover	
	2. The Path of the Beloved	
	3. Good Night—Farewell!	
15.	*Skogsrået* (The Wood-Nymph). Tone-poem for orchestra. MS.	1894
16.	*Vårsång* (Spring Song). Tone-poem.	1894
22.	*Four Legends*.	
	1. Lemminkäinen and the Maidens of Saari	1895, 1897, 1939
	2. The Swan of Tuonela	1893, 1897, 1900
	3. Lemminkäinen in Tuonela	1895, 1897, 1939
	4. Lemminkäinen's Homeward Journey	1895, 1897, 1900
25.	*Scènes historiques*, I.	
	1. All' Overtura	1899
	2. Scena	1899
	3. Festivo	1899, 1911
26.	*Finlandia*. Tone-poem.	1899, 1900
39.	Symphony No. 1 in E minor.	1899
42.	Romance in C major, for strings.	1903
43.	Symphony No. 2 in D major.	1901–2
45.	1. *The Dryad*. Tone-poem	1910
	2. *Dance Intermezzo*	1907
49.	*Pohjola's Daughter*. Symphonic fantasia.	1906

Op.		Date
52.	Symphony No. 3 in C major.	1904–7
53.	*Pan and Echo*. Dance intermezzo.	1906
55.	*Nightride and Sunrise*. Tone-poem.	1907
59.	*In Memoriam*. Funeral march.	1909
63.	Symphony No. 4 in A minor.	1911
64.	*The Bard*. Tone-poem.	1913, 1914
66.	*Scènes historiques*, II.	1912
	1. The Chase, Overture	
	2. Love Song	
	3. At the Drawbridge	
73.	*The Oceanides*. Tone-poem.	1914
82.	Symphony No. 5 in E flat major	1915, 1916, 1919
96.	Three Pieces.	
	1. *Valse lyrique*	1920
	2. *Autrefois, scène pastorale* for two voices and orchestra	1919
	3. *Valse chevaleresque*	1920
98.	(*a*) *Suite mignonne*, for two flutes and strings.	1921
	1. *Petite scène*	
	2. *Polka*	
	3. *Epilogue*	
	(*b*) *Suite champêtre*, for strings.	1921
	1. *Pièce caractéristique*	
	2. *Mélodie élégiaque*	
	3. *Danse*	
100.	*Suite caractéristique*, for harp and strings. MS. (Also in version for piano which is published.)	1922
104.	Symphony No. 6 in D minor.	1923
105.	Symphony No. 7 in C major.	1924
112.	*Tapiola*. Tone-poem.	1926
—	*Presto*, for strings (probably an arrangement of movement from string quartet in B flat, Op. 4). MS.	1889
—	Overture in E.	1890–1
—	*Andantino* and *Menuetto*, for clarinet, two cornets, two horns, baritone and tuba (?). MS.	1890–1
—	*Scène de ballet*. MS.	1891
—	*Karelia* (see also under Op. 10 and Op. 11). MS. Più lento, Moderato assai, Moderato ma non tanto, Vivace, Moderato-Allegro molto-Vivace molto-Maestoso e largamente.	1893

Op.		Date
—	*Andante lirico*, for strings.[1] MS.	1894
—	*Menuetto*. MS.	1894
—	Press Celebrations Music (see Op. 25). MS.	1899
	1. *Praeludium* for clarinet, 2 cornets, 2 horns, baritone and tuba	
	2. Tableau 2, for orchestra: *Andante, ma non troppo lento*	
	3. Tableau 5, for orchestra: *Grave*	
—	*Björneborgarnas March*. MS.	1900
—	*Cortège*. MS.	1901
—	Overture in A minor.[2] MS.	1902
—	*Porträtterna*, for strings (see *Melodramas*). MS.	1906
—	*Scène de ballet* (?).[3] MS.	1909
—	*Promotiomarssi* (Academic March). MS.	1919
—	*Andante festivo* for strings and percussion and for string quartet.	1922

Music for the Theatre

Op.		Date
8.	*Ödlan* (The Lizard) (Lybeck) for solo violin and string quintet. MS.	1909
27.	*King Christian II* (Adolf Paul).	1898
	Elegie, Musette, Menuetto, Fool's Song of the Spider, Nocturne, Serenade, Ballade	
44.	*Kuolema* (Death) (Arvid Järnefelt).	
	Six scenes for strings and percussion. MS.	1903
	No. 1 rev. as Valse triste	1904
	Nos. 3 and 4 rev, as Scene with Cranes. MS.	1906
62.	(*a*) Canzonetta for strings.	1911
	(*b*) Valse romantique, for strings.	1911
	(Both from Incidental Music to *Kuolema*.)	
46.	*Pelléas et Mélisande* (Maeterlinck).	1905
	At the Castle Gate, Mélisande, By the Seashore, By a Spring in the Park, The Three Blind Sisters, Pastorale, Mélisande at the Spinning-Wheel, Entr'acte, The Death of Mélisande	

---

[1] Probably the same as the *Impromptu* for strings (often cited as Op. 87a) and an arrangement of the fifth and sixth of the *Impromptus* for piano, Op. 5.

[2] Hitherto believed to have been written in 1890–1, but Johnson and Furuhjelm have arrived at the later date.

[3] Johnson asserts the existence of this work, but nowhere does he appear to offer any evidence of its independence from the earlier work of the same name.

Op.		Date
51.	*Belshazzar's Feast* (Hjalmar Procopé).	1906
	Original score: 1. Alla marcia, 2. Nocturne, 3. The Jewish Girl's Song, 4. Allegretto, 5. Dance of Life, 6. Dance of Death, 7. Tempo sostenuto, 8. Allegro. MS.	
	Concert Suite, composed of following numbers: 1. (entitled Oriental Procession), 3. (Solitude), 2. (Night Music), 5. and 6. (Khadra's Dance)	
54.	*Swanwhite* (Strindberg).	1908
	Original score: 14 scenes. MS.	
	Concert Suite: The Peacock, The Harp, The Maiden with the Roses, Listen! the Robin sings, The Prince Alone, Swanwhite and the Prince, Song of Praise	
71.	*Scaramouche* (Poul Knudsen).	1913
83.	*Jedermann* (Everyman) (Hugo von Hofmannsthal) for mixed chorus, piano, organ and orchestra. MS.	1916
109.	*The Tempest* (Shakespeare).	1926
	Original score in 34 parts, for soloists, mixed chorus, harmonium and orchestra. MS.	
	Concert score:	
	No. 1. Prelude	
	No. 2. Suite I: The Oak-tree, Humoresque, Caliban's Song, The Harvesters, Canon, Scena, Intrada-Berceuse, Entr'acte, Ariel's Song, The Storm	
	No. 3. Suite II: Chorus of the Winds, Intermezzo, Dance of the Nymphs, Prospero, Song I, Song II, Miranda, The Naiads, Dance Episode.	
—	*Näcken* (The Watersprite) (Wennerberg). MS.	1888
	Two songs with piano trio	
—	*The Language of the Birds* (Adolf Paul). MS.	1911
	Wedding March for Act III.	

Solo Instrument and Orchestra

47.	Concerto in D minor, for violin and orchestra.	1903, 1905
69.	Two Serenades, for violin and orchestra.	
	No. 1 in D	1912
	No. 2 in G minor	1913

Op.		*Date*
77.	Two Pieces, for violin (or cello) and orchestra. 1. *Cantique* (*Laetare anima mea*) 2. *Devotion* (*Ab imo pectore*)	1914
87.	Two Humoresques, for violin and orchestra. No. 1 in D minor No. 2 in D major	1917
89.	Four Humoresques, for violin and orchestra (often numbered 3–6). No. 1 in G minor (string orchestra) No. 2 in G minor (string orchestra) No. 3 in E flat (for orchestra) No. 4 in G minor	1917

BRASS ENSEMBLE

—	*Tiera.* Tone-poem for brass *ensemble* and percussion.	1898

CHAMBER MUSIC

—	Octet for flute, clarinet and strings (material subsequently used in the 1893 version of *En Saga*). MS.	1891
—	Quintet in G minor for piano and strings. MS.	1889–90
4.	String quartet in B flat major. MS.	1890
56.	String quartet in D minor (*Voces intimae*).	1909
—	String quartet in E flat major. MS.	1885
—	String quartet in A minor. MS.	1889
—	Theme and variations in C sharp minor, for string quartet. MS.	1888
—	Fugue, for string quartet. MS.	1888
—	Adagio, for string quartet. MS.	?
—	Quartet for violin, cello, harmonium and piano. MS.	Before 1885
—	Quartet in E minor for piano, two violins and cello. MS.	1881–2
—	Quartet in C major for piano, two violins and cello. MS.	1891
—	Suite in G minor, for string trio. MS.	1885
—	Suite in A major, for string trio. MS.	1889
—	Piano trio in A minor. MS.	1881–2
—	Piano trio (the so-called *Korpo* trio). MS.	1887
—	Piano trio in C major (*Loviisa* trio). MS.	1888

Appendix B—Catalogue of Works

Violin and Piano

Op.		*Date*
2.	Romance and Epilogue.	1888, rev. 1912
78.	Four Pieces for violin (or cello) and piano.	
	1. Impromptu	1915
	2. Romance	1915
	3. Religioso	1919
	4. Rigaudon	1915
79.	Six Pieces.	1915
	Souvenir, Tempo di menuetto, Danse caractéristique, Sérénade, Danse idyll, Berceuse	
80.	Sonatina in E major.	1915
81.	Five Pieces.	1915
	Mazurka, Rondino, Waltz, Aubade, Menuetto	
102.	Novelette.	1923
106.	Five *Danses champêtres*.	1925
115.	Four Pieces.	1929
	On the Heath, Ballade, Humoresque, The Bells	
116.	Three Pieces.	1929
	1. Scène de danse	
	2. Danse caractéristique	
	3. Rondeau romantique	
—	Sonata in D minor. MS.	1881–2
—	Sonata in F major. MS.	1889
—	Andante cantabile. MS.	1887

Violin and Cello

—	*Vattendroppar* (Water Drops). MS.	1875–6

Violin and Kantele

—	*Kehtolaulu* (Lullaby).	1899

Violin and Viola

—	Duo, MS.	1886

Viola and Piano

—	Rondo. MS.	1893

Appendix B—Catalogue of Works

Cello and Piano

Op.		*Date*
20.	Malinconia.	1901
—	Andantino. MS.	1884
—	Fantasia. MS.	1899–1900

Organ

Op.		*Date*
111.	Two Pieces.	
	Intrada	1925
	Sorgemusik (Funeral Music)	1931

Piano Music

Op.		*Date*
5.	Six Impromptus.	1893
12.	Sonata in F major.	1893
24.	Ten Pieces.	
	Impromptu	1894
	Romance in A	1894
	Caprice	1895
	Romance in D minor	1895
	Waltz in E	1895
	Idyll	1898
	Andantino	1898
	Nocturno	1900
	Romance in D flat	1903
	Barcarola	1903
34.	Ten Pieces.	1914–16
	Waltz, Dance air, Mazurka, Humorous, Drollery, Rêverie, Pastoral Dance, The Harper, Reconnaissance, Souvenir	
40.	*Pensées lyriques.*	1912–14
	Valsette, Chant sans paroles, Humoresque, Menuetto, Berceuse, Pensée mélodique, Rondoletto, Scherzando, Petite Sérénade, Polonaise	
41.	*Kyllikki:* three lyric pieces.	1904
	Largamente—Allegro	
	Andantino	
	Commodo	

Op.		*Date*
58.	Ten Pieces.	1909
	Rêverie, Scherzino, Air varié, The Shepherd, The Evening, Dialogue, Tempo di menuetto, Fisher Song, Sérénade, Summer Song	
67.	Three Sonatinas.	1912
	No. 1, in F sharp minor	
	No. 2, in E	
	No. 3, in B flat minor	
68.	Two Rondinos.	1912
	No. 1, in G sharp minor	
	No. 2, in C sharp minor	
74.	Four Lyric Pieces.	1914
	Eclogue, Soft West Wind, At the Dance, In the Old Home	
75.	Five Pieces.	1914
	When the Mountain-Ash is in Flower, The Lonely Fir, The Aspen, The Birch, The Fir	
76.	Thirteen Pieces.	1914
	Esquisse, Étude, Carillon, Humoresque, Consolation, Romanzetta, Affettuoso, Pièce enfantine, Arabesque, Elegiaco, Linnea, Capriccietto, Harlequinade	
85.	Five Pieces.	1916
	Bellis, Oeillet, Iris, Aquileja, Campanula	
94.	Six Pieces.	1919
	Dance, Novelette, Sonnett, Berger et Bergerette, Mélodie, Gavotte	
97.	Six Bagatelles.	1920
	Humoresque I, Song, Little Waltz, Humorous March, Impromptu, Humoresque II	
99.	Eight Pieces.	1922
	Pièce humoristique, Esquisse, Souvenir, Impromptu, Couplet, Animoso, Moment de Valse, Petite Marche	
101.	Five Romantic Pieces.	1923
	Romance, Chant du soir, Scène lyrique, Humoresque, Scène romantique	
103.	Five Characteristic Impressions.	1924
	The Village Church, The Fiddler, The Oarsman, The Storm, In Mournful Mood	
114.	Five Esquisses. MS.	1929
	Landscape, Winter Scene, Forest Lake, Song in the Forest, Spring Vision	

Op. *Date*

— *Au crépuscule.* MS. 1887
— Andantino. MS. 1888
— Scherzo. MS. 1888?
— Allegretto. MS. 1889
— *Florestan.* Suite in four movements: Moderato, Molto moderato, Andante, Tempo primo. MS. 1889
— *Kavaljeren* (The cavalier). 1900
— Finnish Folk Songs (arr.). 1903
  1. *Minun kultani* (My beloved)
  2. *Sydämestäni rakastan* (I love you with all my heart)
  3. *Ilta tulee* (Evening comes)
  4. *Tuopa tyttö, kaunis tyttö* (That beautiful girl)
  5. *Velisurmaaja* (The fratricide)
  6. *Häämuistelma* (Wedding memories)
— *Spagnuolo.* 1913
— *Till trånaden* (To longing). 1913
— *Mandolinata.* 1917
— *Morceau romantique sur un motif de M. Jacob de Julin* (also known as *Pièce romantique*). 1925

Songs

1. Five Christmas Songs, with piano. 1895, 1913
  1. *Nu står jul vid snöig port* (Topelius) (Now Christmas stands at the snowy gate)
  2. *Nu så kommer julen* (Topelius) (Now Christmas has come)
  3. *Det mörknar ute* (Topelius) (Outside it is growing dark)
  4. *Giv mig ej glans, ej guld, ej prakt* (Topelius) (Give me no splendour, gold or pomp)
  5. *On hangket korkeat* (Joukahainen) (High are the snowdrifts)

3. *Arioso* (Runeberg).
  (*a*) With piano 1893
  (*b*) With string orchestra 1913

13. Seven Songs (Runeberg), with piano.
  1. *Under strandens granar* (Under the fir-trees) 1892
  2. *Kyssens hopp* (The kiss's hope) 1892

Op.		Date
	3. *Hjärtats morgon* (The heart's morning)	1891
	4. *Våren flyktar hastigt* (Spring flies speedily)	1891
	With orchestra. MS.	1914
	5. *Drömmen* (The dream)	1891
	6. *Till Frigga* (To Frigga)	1892
	7. *Jägargossen* (The young huntsman)	1891
17.	Seven Songs, with piano.	
	1. *Se'n har jag ej frågat mera* (Runeberg) (Since then I have questioned no further)	
	With orchestra.	1903
	2. *Sov in!* (Tavaststjerna) (Sleep on!)	1894
	With orchestra. MS.	
	3. *Fågellek* (Tavaststjerna) (Enticement)	1891
	With orchestra. MS.	
	4. *Vilse* (Tavaststjerna) (Astray)	1894
	5. *En slända* (Levertin) (A dragon-fly)	1894
	With orchestra. MS.	
	6. *Illalle* (Forsman-Koskimies) (To evening)	1898
	7. *Lastu lainehilla* (Calamnius) (Driftwood)	1898
33.	*Koskenlaskijan morsiamet* (Oksanen) (The ferryman's brides), for baritone or mezzo-soprano and orchestra.	1897
35.	1. Two Songs, with piano.	1907–8
	1. *Jubal* (Josephson)	
	With orchestra. MS.	
	2. *Teodora* (Gripenberg)	
36.	Six Songs, with piano.	1899
	1. *Svarta Rosor* (Josephson) (Black roses)	
	2. *Men min fågel märks dock icke* (Runeberg) (But my bird is long in homing)	
	3. *Bollspelet vid Trianon* (Fröding) (Tennis at Trianon)	
	With orchestra. MS.	
	4. *Säv, säv, susa* (Fröding) (Sigh, rushes, sigh)	
	5. *Marssnön* (Wecksell) (The March snow)	
	6. *Demanten på marssnön* (Wecksell) (The diamond on the March snow)	
	With orchestra. MS.	
37.	Five Songs, with piano.	
	1. *Den första kyssen* (Runeberg) (The first kiss)	1898

Appendix B—Catalogue of Works

Op.		Date

2. *Lasse liten* (Topelius) (Little Lasse) 1898
3. *Soluppgång* (Hedberg) (Sunrise) 1898
   With orchestra. MS.
4. *Var det en dröm?* (Wecksell) (Was it a dream?) 1902
5. *Flickan kom ifrån sin älsklings möte* (Runeberg) (The maid came from her lover's tryst) 1901
   With orchestra. MS.

38. Five Songs, with piano.
1. *Höstkväll* (Rydberg) (Autumn evening) 1903
   With orchestra.
2. *På verandan vid havet* (Rydberg) (On a balcony by the sea) 1902
   With orchestra. MS.
3. *I natten* (Rydberg) (In the night) 1903
   With orchestra. MS.
4. *Harpolekaren och hans son* (Rydberg) (The harper and his son) 1904
5. *Jag ville jag vore i Indialand* (Fröding) (I would I were in India) 1904

50. Six Songs, with piano. 1906
1. *Lenzgesang* (Fitger) (Spring song)
2. *Sehnsucht* (Weiss) (Longing)
3. *Im Feld ein Mädchen singt* (Susman) (In the field a maid sings)
4. *Aus banger Brust* (Dehmel) (From anxious heart)
   With orchestra. MS.
5. *Die stille Stadt* (Dehmel) (The silent city)
6. *Rosenlied* (Ritter) (Song of the roses)

57. Eight Songs (Josephson), with piano. 1909
1. *Älvan och snigeln* (The elf and the snail)
2. *En blomma stod vid vägen* (A flower stood by the wayside)
3. *Kvarnhjulet* (The mill-wheel)
4. *Maj* (May)
5. *Jag är ett träd* (I am a tree)
6. *Hertig Magnus* (Duke Magnus)
7. *Vänskapens blomma* (The flower of friendship)
8. *Näcken* (The watersprite)

60. Two Songs from Shakespeare's *Twelfth Night*, with piano or guitar. 1909
1. *Kom nu hit, död* (Come away, Death)
   With strings and harp. MS. 1957

Op.		*Date*
	2. *Och när som jag var en liten smådräng* (When that I was and a little tiny boy)	
61.	Eight Songs, with piano.	1910
	1. *Långsamt som kvällskyn* (Tavaststjerna) (Slowly as the evening sun)	
	2. *Vattenplask* (Rydberg) (Lapping waters)	
	3. *När jag drömmer* (Tavaststjerna) (When I dream)	
	4. *Romeo* (Tavaststjerna)	
	5. *Romance* (Tavaststjerna)	
	6. *Dolce far niente* (Tavaststjerna)	
	7. *Fåfäng önskan* (Runeberg) (Idle wishes)	
	8. *Vårtagen* (Gripenberg) (Spring spell)	
70.	*Luonnotar.* Tone-poem for soprano and orchestra.	1913
72.	Six Songs, with piano.	
	1. *Vi ses igen* (Rydberg) (Farewell)	1914
	2. *Orions bälte* (Topelius) (Orion's girdle)	1914
	3. *Kyssen* (Rydberg) (The kiss)	1915
	4. *Kaiutar* (Larin Kyösti) (The echo nymph)	1915
	5. *Der Wanderer und der Bach* (Greif) (The wayfarer and the stream)	1915
	6 *Hundra vägar* (Runeberg) (A hundred ways)	1907
86.	Six Songs, with piano.	1916
	1. *Vårförnimmelser* (Tavaststjerna) (The coming of spring)	
	2. *Längtan heter min arvedel* (Karlfeldt) (Longing is my heritage)	
	3. *Dold förening* (Snoilsky) (Hidden union)	
	4. *Och finns det en tanke?* (Tavaststjerna) (And is there a thought?)	
	5. *Sångarlön* (Snoilsky) (The singer's reward)	
	6. *I systrar, I bröder* (Lybeck) (Ye sisters, ye brothers)	
88.	Six Songs, with piano.	1917
	1. *Blåsippan* (Franzén) (The blue anemone)	
	2. *De bägge rosorna* (Franzén) (The two roses)	
	3. *Vitsippan* (Franzén) (The star-flower)	
	4. *Sippan* (Runeberg) (The anemone)	
	5. *Törnet* (Runeberg) (The thorn)	
	6. *Blommans öde* (Runeberg) (The flower's destiny)	
90.	Six Songs (Runeberg), with piano.	1917
	1. *Norden* (The north)	
	2. *Hennes budskap* (Her message)	
	3. *Morgonen* (The morning)	

Op.		Date
	4. *Fågelfängaren* (The bird-catcher)	
	5. *Sommarnatten* (Summer night)	
	6. *Vem stryde hit din väg?* (Who brought you hither?)	
—	*Erloschen* (Busse-Palmo), with piano. (Lost.)	1906
—	*Narcissen* (Gripenberg), with piano.	1918
—	*Segeln* (Öhqvist), with piano. (The sails.)	1899
—	*Serenade* (Runeberg), with piano.	1888
—	*Serenade* (Stagnelius), with orchestra. MS.	1895
—	*Små flickorna* (Procopé) with piano. (The little girls.)	1920
—	*Souda, souda, sinisorsa* (Koskimies) (Swim, duck, swim).	1899
—	Hymn to Thais (Borgström), with piano.	1900

Vocal Duet

—	*Tanken* (Runeberg) (The thought), for two sopranos and piano. MS.	1915

Choral Music

7.	*Kullervo,* symphonic poem for soprano, baritone, male chorus and orchestra (based on the *Kalevala*). MS.	1892
	1. Introduction	
	2. Kullervo's Youth	
	3. Kullervo and his Sister	
	4. Kullervo goes to War	
	5. Kullervo's Death	
14.	*Rakastava* (The Lover), for male chorus *a cappella* (from Book I of the *Kanteletar*).	1893
	1. *Missä armahani?* (Where is my beloved?) from Canto 173	
	2. *Armahan kulku* (My beloved's way) from Canto 174	
	3. *Hyvää iltaa, lintuseni* (Good evening, my little bird) from Canto 122	
	With string orchestra. MS.	1894
	For mixed chorus *a cappella.*	1898
	(See also *Orchestral Works.*)	

Op. *Date*

18. Nine Part-songs, for male chorus *a cappella.*
    1. *Isänmaalle* (Cajander) (To the Fatherland) 1900
       Also for mixed chorus.
    2. *Veljeni vierailla mailla* (Aho) (My brothers abroad) 1904
    3. *Saarella palaa*[1] (Book I of the *Kanteletar*, Canto 186) (Fire on the Island) 1895
       For mixed chorus *a cappella.* 1898
    4. *Min rastas raataa* (Book I of the *Kanteletar*, Canto 219) (Busy as a thrush) 1898
       Also for mixed chorus *a cappella.* 1898
    5. *Metsämiehen laulu* (Kivi) (The Woodman's song) 1898
    6. *Sydameni laulu* (Kivi) (The Song of my heart) 1898
       For mixed chorus *a cappella.* 1907
    7. *Sortunut ääni* (Book I of the *Kanteletar*, Canto 57) (The broken voice) 1898
       For mixed chorus *a cappella.* 1898
    8. *Terve kuu* (*Kalevala,* Runo XLIX, 403–23) (Hail! Moon) 1901
    9. *Venematka* (*Kalevala,* Runo XL, 1–16) (The boat journey) 1893
       Also for mixed chorus *a cappella.*
19. *Impromptu,* for women's chorus and orchestra (Rydberg).[2] 1902, 1910
21. *Natus in curas,* for male chorus *a cappella* (Gustafsson). 1896
23. Cantata for the University Ceremonies of 1897, for soloists, mixed chorus and orchestra (Koskimies). 1897
    Excerpts for Mixed Chorus.
    1. *Me nuoriso Suomen* (We, the youth of Finland)
    2. *Tuuli tuudittele* (The wind rocks)
    3. *Oi toivo, toivo, sä lietomieli* (Oh Hope, Hope, you dreamer)
    4. *Montapa elon merellä* (Many on the sea of life)
    5. *Sammuva sainio mean* (The fading thoughts of the Earth)
    6. (*a*) *Soi kiitokseksi Luojan* (Let thanks ring to the Lord)
       (*b*) *Tuule, tuule leppeämmin* (Blow, blow gentler)
    7. *Lempi, sun valtas ääretön on* (Love, your realm is vast)
    8. *Kuin virta vuolas* (As the swift current)

---

[1] Also known as *Työnsa kumpasellaki* (Each had his work).

[2] Also known as *Lifslust* and *Gossar och flickor*, and in this country as *Thou who guidest the stars.*

Op. *Date*

9. *Oi kallis Suomi, äiti verraton* (Oh, Precious Finland, mother beyond compare)

28. *Sandels*, improvisation for male chorus and orchestra (Runeberg). MS. 1898, 1915

31. 1. *Laulu Lemminkäiselle* (Veijola) (A Song for Lemminkainen) for male chorus and orchestra. 1900
    2. *Har du mod?* (Wecksell) (Have you courage?) for male chorus and orchestra. 1904
    3. *Atenarnes sång* (Rydberg). (The Song of the Athenians) for boys' and mens' voices, saxhorn septet, triangle, bass drum and cymbals (alt. accomp. wind band). 1899

32. *Tulen synty* for baritone, male chorus and orchestra (*Kalevala*, Runo XLVII, 41–110) (*The Origin of Fire*).[1] 1902, 1910

48. *Vapautettu kuningatar*, cantata for mixed chorus and orchestra (Cajander) (The liberated queen).[2] 1906

65. Two Part-songs for mixed chorus *a cappella.*
    1. *Män från slätten och havet* (Knape) (Men from land and sea) 1911
    2. *Klockmelodin i Berghälls kyrka* (Engström) (Church bells of Berghäll) 1912

84. Five Part-songs for chorus *a cappella.*
    1. *Herr Lager* (Fröding) 1914
    2. *På berget* (Gripenberg) (On the mountain) 1915
    3. *Ett drömackord* (Fröding) (A dream chord) 1915
    4. *Evige Eros* (Gripenberg) (Eternal Eros) 1915
    5. *Till havs* (Reuter) (To sea) 1915

91. 1. *March of the Finnish Jäger Battalion.* For male chorus and orchestra (Nurmio). 1917
       Also for male chorus *a cappella.*
       Also for orchestra.
    2. *Scout March.* For mixed chorus *a cappella* (Finne-Procopé).[3] 1917
       Also with orchestral accompaniment.

---

[1] Also known as *Ukko the Firemaker.*

[2] Composed to a German translation of Cajander and published as *Die gefangene Königin* (The captive Queen); also known as *Siell' laulavi kuningatar* (There sings the Queen) and *Snellmans Fest kantat.*

[3] Also known as *Det danske Spejderes March* (The Danish Scout March).

Op. *Date*

92. *Oma maa* (Our native land). Cantata for mixed chorus and orchestra (Kallio). 1918
93. *Jordens sång* (Song of the Earth). Cantata for mixed chorus and orchestra (Hemmer), written for the inauguration of Åbo Akademi. 1919
95. *Maan virsi* (Hymn of the Earth). Cantata for mixed chorus and orchestra (Leino). 1920
107. Hymn, for chorus with organ. MS. 1925
108. Two Part-songs for male chorus *a cappella* (Kyösti). 1925
    1. *Humoreski*
    2. *Ne pitkän matkan kulkijat* (Wanderers on the long way)
110. *Väinön virsi* (Väinö's Song). For mixed chorus and orchestra (*Kalevala*, Runo XLIII, 385–422).
113. *Masonic Ritual Music*, for male voices, piano and organ.
    1. Introduction, 2. *Thoughts by our Comfort* (Schiller), 3. Introduction and Hymn, 4. *Marcia* (Goethe), 5. *Light* (Simelius), 6. *Salem* (Rydberg), 7. *Whosoever has a love* (Rydberg) (All) 1927
    8. *Ode to Fraternity* (Sario) 1946
    9. Hymn (Sario) 1946
    10. *Marche funèbre* 1927
    11. Ode (Korpela) 1927
    12. *Finlandia Hymn* (Sola) 1928

    All revised 1948

— University Cantata, for mixed chorus and orchestra (Leino). MS. 1894
  Juhlamarssi (Festive March), for mixed chorus *a cappella* (Leino)

— Cantata for the Coronation of Nicholas II, for soloists, mixed chorus and orchestra (Cajander). MS. 1896

— *Työkansan marssi* (Workers' March), for mixed chorus *a cappella* (Erkko). 1896

— *Päiv' ei pääse* (The day is not ended), for children's voices *a cappella*.[1] 1896

— *Carminalia*, three Latin Songs for students arranged for soprano, alto and bass *a cappella* or soprano and alto with piano and harmonium (texts collected by Elise Stenbäck). 1899
  1. *Ecce novum gaudium*. 2. *Angelus emittitur*. 3. *In stadio laboris*.

---

[1] Also known as *Aamusumussa*.

Op.		*Date*
—	*Till Thérèse Hahl* (To Thérèse Hahl), for mixed chorus *a cappella* (Tawasastjerna).[1]	1902
—	*Kotikaipaus* (Nostalgia), for three women's voices *a cappella* (von Konow).	1902
—	*Ej med klagan* (Not with lamentation), for mixed chorus *a cappella* (Runeberg).[2]	1905
—	*Kansakoululaisten marssi* (March of the elementary school children), for children's voices *a cappella* (Onnen Pekka).[3]	1910
—	Cantata to words of von Konow for women's chorus *a cappella.*	1911
—	*Drömmarna* (The dreams), for mixed chorus *a cappella* (Reuter).	1912
—	*Uusmaalaisten laulu* (Song of the people of Uusimaa), for mixed chorus *a cappella* (Terhi).	1912
	Also for male chorus *a cappella.*	
—	Three Songs for American Schools.	1913
	1. Autumn song (Dixon). 2. The Sun upon the lake is low (Scott). 3. A cavalry march (Macleod).	
—	*Kuutamolla* (In the moonlight) for male chorus *a cappella* (Suonio).	1916
—	*Fridolinsdårskap* (Fridolin's madness), for male chorus *a cappella* (Karlfeldt).	1917
—	*Jone havsfärd* (Jonah's journey), for male chorus *a cappella* (Karlfeldt).	1918
—	Two Songs (Schybergson), for male chorus *a cappella.*	1918
	1. *Ute hörs stormen* (Outside the storm is raging)	
	2. *Brusande rusar en våg* (The roaring of a wave)	
—	*Viipurin Lauli-Veikoojen kunniamarssi* (March of the singing brothers of Viipuri), for male chorus *a cappella* (Eerola).	1920
—	*Likhet* (Resemblance), for male chorus *a cappella* (Runeberg).	1922
—	*Koulutie* (The way to school), for children's voices *a cappella* (Koskenniemi).	1925
—	*Johdantovuorolauluja* (Antiphons) for mixed chorus.	1925
	1. *Palmusunnuntaina* (Palm Sunday)	
	2. *Phyhäinpäivänä* (All Saints Day)	
	3. *Rukouspäivänä* (General Prayers)	

---

[1] Also known as *Lauloit piennä.*

[2] Alternative title *Till minnet av Albert Edelfelt.*

[3] Also known as *Uno Cygnaeksen muistolle.*

Op.		*Date*
—	*Suur' olet, Herra* (You are mighty, O Lord), hymn for mixed chorus *a cappella* (Korpela). Also for male chorus.	1927
—	*Siltavahti* (The guardian of the bridge), March for male chorus *a cappella* (written for the New York *Laulu-Miehet*). MS.	1929
—	*Karjalan osa* for male chorus (Nurminen).	1930

OPERAS

—	*Veneen luominen* (The building of the boat). Sketches only (to a libretto of Sibelius himself).	1893
—	*Jungfrun i tornet* (The maiden in the tower). Opera in one act (to a libretto of Raf. Herzberg). MS.	1896

MELODRAMAS

15.	*Skogsrået* (The wood-nymph). For piano, two horns and string orchestra to accompany verses by Rydberg. (See also *Orchestral Works.*) MS.[1]	1894
29.	*Snöfrid.* Improvisation for speaker, mixed chorus and orchestra to accompany verses by Rydberg.[1]	1896
30.	*Islossningen i Uleå älv* (The melting of the ice on the Uleå River). Improvisation for speaker, male chorus and orchestra. MS.[1]	1898
—	*Trånaden* (Longing), for piano to accompany the recitation of verses by Stagnelius. MS.	1887
—	*Svartsjukans nätter* (Nights of jealousy), for violin, cello and piano to accompany the recitation of verses by Runeberg. MS.	1888
—	*Grefvinnans konterfej* (The countess's portrait) for string orchestra to accompany the verses of Topelius. MS. (See *Orchestral Works*: *Porträtterna*, for strings.)	1906
—	*Ett ensamt skidspår* (A lonely ski trail), for piano to accompany verses by Gripenberg.	1925
	Arr. for harp and strings. MS.	1948

[1] Piano reductions of all these works have been published.

APPENDIX C

PERSONALIA

Ackté, Aino (1876–1944), Finnish soprano. She made her début as Marguerite in *Faust* at the Opéra and sang frequently in Paris and at the Metropolitan Opera, New York, during the early years of the present century. In 1911 she and Fazer were instrumental in founding the Finnish Opera, where she sang many leading roles. She became its director in 1938. Some idea of her *tessitura* and her brilliance can be gained from *Luonnotar*, which Sibelius wrote for her.

Ahlqvist, August Engelbrekt (1826–89), Finnish poet and philologist. For many years professor of Finnish at Helsinki University, he published his poetry under the pseudonym Oksanen.

Becker, Albert Ernst Anton (1834–99), German composer and theorist. From 1881 until his death Becker taught composition at the Scharwenka Conservatoire, Berlin.

Bobrikov, Nikolai Ivanovich (1839–1904), Russian governor-general of Finland from 1898 until his death. His period of rule marked a distinct hardening of Russia's attitude to Finland, and these oppressive years, known as the *ofärdsåren*, are identified with Bobrikov's policies. He was assassinated in 1904 in the Finnish Senate.

Cajander, Paul Emil (1846–1913), Finnish poet and translator. Lecturer in Finnish at Helsinki University from 1890 until 1912. His work as a translator overshadowed his original work and his poems were not collected until after his death. He is best known for his Finnish translation of Shakespeare, but he also translated Runeberg, Topelius and Wecksell from the Swedish.

Damrosch, Walter (1862–1950), German-born conductor and composer who settled in America. He conducted the New York Philharmonic and other American orchestras and was for some years musical adviser to the N.B.C. He included a number of Sibelius works in his programmes, and commissioned *Tapiola*.

Appendix C—Personalia

Downes, Olin (1886–1955), American music critic, first of the *Boston Post* and subsequently the *New York Times*. An expert on Sibelius, he was awarded the Order of the White Rose of Finland, and when the composer's seventy-fifth birthday was celebrated in a broadcast, Downes was chosen as speaker and Toscanini as conductor. His writings include *The Lure of Music* (1918), *Symphonic Broadcasts* (1932) and *Symphonic Masterpieces* (1936).

Ekman, Ida (1875–1942), Finnish soprano. She studied at the Helsinki Music Institute and in Vienna and Paris, where she sang when the Finnish orchestra visited the French capital in 1900. After engagements at the Nuremberg opera she left the stage to devote herself to *Lieder*. She was the first Finnish singer to introduce Sibelius's songs to the Continent.

Ekman, Karl (1895–), Finnish writer on music, son of the above. His father was a pianist and conductor, who studied with Busoni and was a friend of Sibelius. Karl Ekman published a biography of Sibelius in 1935, which appeared in England the following year.

Faltin, Friedrich Richard (1835–1918), Finnish musician of German origin who was for many years a dominant figure in Finnish musical life. After teaching at Viipuri (Viborg) he took up an appointment in Helsinki as conductor of the *Nya Teaterns Orkester* and organist of the Nicolai church. Together with Wegelius he took part in the foundation of the Helsinki Music Institute.

Flodin, Karl Theodore (1858–1918), Finnish critic and composer. A pupil of Faltin, he subsequently studied in Leipzig before acting as a critic in Helsinki during the latter part of the nineteenth century. He left the *Helsingfors Posten* in 1908, and spent the last years of his life in Buenos Aires.

Fougstedt, Nils-Erik (1910–), Finnish composer and conductor, since 1944 conductor of the Finnish Radio Orchestra. His works include three symphonies, a cello concerto, and chamber music.

Fröding, Gustaf (1860–1911), Swedish poet from Värmland in Central Sweden. After studying at Upsala, which he left without taking a degree, he returned to Värmland. His nervous health was precarious, and he spent over six years in Upsala hospital. In early years he was influenced by Goethe, Heine, Byron and Burns. One of his most important stylistic features is a skilful use of alliteration and assonance, as well as the mastery of rhythm which gives his poetry its distinct musical character. One of his most famous lyrics, *Ingalill*, was set by Sibelius and is known by its opening words, *Säf, säf, susa.*

Fuchs, Robert (1847–1927), Austrian composer and teacher. Fuchs studied in Vienna, where he taught composition from 1875 until 1912. His works include operas, *Die Königsbraut* (1889), *Die Teufelsglocken* (1892), choral works, three symphonies and a quantity of chamber music.

Furuhjelm, Erik Gustav (1883–), Finnish composer and critic. Furuhjelm studied with Wegelius and then with Robert Fuchs in Vienna. His work includes two symphonies and chamber music. He was for many years active as a critic for *Dagens Tidning*, and the author of *Jean Sibelius, hans tondiktning och drag ur hans liv* (1915), a pioneer study of the composer.

Gallén-Kallela, Axel (1865–1931), Finnish painter who, like Sibelius, was inspired by the legends recounted in the *Kalevala.*

Goldmark, Karl (1830–1915), Austro-Hungarian composer and teacher. Best known nowadays for his *Rustic Wedding* symphony, the overture *In Spring* and the first of his two violin concertos, he also wrote six operas, two on English subjects.

Gripenberg, Bertil (1878–1947), Finnish poet. After the publication of some early erotic poems he became one of the mouthpieces of Finnish nationalism in the early years of this century, and took part in the Finnish war of independence in 1918. He was also a vigorous supporter of the cause of the Swedish-speaking minority of Finland.

Järnefelt, Armas (1869–1958), Finnish composer and conductor. Sibelius's brother-in-law. After studies in Helsinki with Wegelius and Busoni, Järnefelt went to Berlin and then to Paris, where he studied with Massenet. From 1907 until 1932 he was conductor of the Royal Opera, Stockholm, after which he held conducting appointments in Helsinki. He was famous in the Scandinavian countries as a Beethoven conductor and for his readings of Mozart and Wagner operas. As a composer his larger works were overshadowed by the popularity of the *Berceuse* and *Praeludium.*

Järnefelt, Arvid (1861–1932), Finnish author. Brother of above. He was much influenced by Tolstoy, whose theories he attempted to apply in Finland. His output includes several plays and novels, many of which are patriotic in character.

Josephson, Ernst Abraham (1851–1906), Swedish painter and poet. After studies in Stockholm he went to Paris, where he came under the influence of Manet. He spent most of his life in France, and made visits to Italy and

Spain. His collections of verse include *Svarta rosor* (1888) and *Gula rosor* (1896).

Kajanus, Robert (1856–1933), Finnish conductor and composer. He began his studies at Helsinki with Talsin and Niemann, continuing in Leipzig under Hans Richter. After studies in Paris with Svendsen he returned in 1882 to found the Helsinki Philharmonic Society Orchestra, who gave regular concerts devoted to the standard classics. In 1900 he toured the principal European capitals with the orchestra. In 1919 he initiated the Nordic Music Festival, which since then has become a triennial event. He was the foremost Sibelius interpreter of his time, and made a number of historic recordings in the thirties subsidized by the Finnish Government. Sibelius dedicated *Pohjola's Daughter* to him. As a composer he wrote a modest quantity of music, including the *Aino* symphony, two Finnish rhapsodies and a sinfonietta.

Karlfeldt, Erik Axel (1864–1931), Swedish poet from Dalecarlia. Generally regarded as the leading poet of his day, and for many years secretary of the Swedish Academy. He was awarded the Nobel Prize for Literature posthumously in 1931.

Koussevitzky, Serge (1875–1951), Russian conductor. He began his career as a virtuoso double-bass player, in which capacity he appeared in London in 1907. He studied Nikisch's methods in Berlin and founded an orchestra in Russia. He left Russia after the Revolution, and in 1924 accepted the conductorship of the Boston Symphony Orchestra, which he held until his death. He was undoubtedly one of the greatest conductors of the twentieth century, and championed a number of Sibelius's orchestral works, many of which he recorded. His reading of the seventh symphony is particularly outstanding.

Lambert, Constant (1905–51), English composer, conductor and critic. His most outstanding works are *Summer's Last Will and Testament* and the popular *Horoscope* and *Rio Grande*. A brilliant ballet conductor, he directed the first performances of many new works and increased the appreciation of ballet in the thirties and forties. His book, *Music Ho!*, which deals appreciatively with Sibelius, was an influential factor in the 'cult' of Sibelius during the thirties.

Lönnrot, Elias (1802–84), Lönnrot collected a vast quantity of folk-literature during the first half of the nineteenth century, and published numerous key-works in Finnish literature, including *Kantele* (1829–31), poems and songs collected in the Finnish Karelia, the more celebrated *Kalevala* (1835–1836) and a collection of lyrics called *Kanteletar* (1840).

Lybeck, Mikael (1864–1925), Finnish poet, novelist and dramatist. One of the finest lyrical poets of the nineties in Finland, the *ofärdsåren*, when Russia increased her pressure on Finnish life; many of his poems express the anxieties of those years. His plays include a study of Schopenhauer and *Ödlan* (The Lizard), to which Sibelius provided music.

Marx, Adolf Bernhard (1795–1866), German scholar, author and composer. His most important work is the four-volume *Lehre von der musikalischen Composition* (Leipzig, 1837–47). He also published a study of Beethoven's keyboard music.

Newmarch, Rosa (1857–1940), English writer on music. She visited Russia in 1897 and worked at the Imperial Public Library in St Petersburg under Vladimir Stassov. She was an energetic champion of Russian and Czech music, publishing studies of Tchaikovsky and Borodin and a translation of Hoffmeister's book on Dvořák. She was a prolific writer of programme notes and also the author of a history of Czech music. She corresponded with Sibelius for many years and did a great deal to popularize his music in England.

Oksanen. See *Ahlqvist*.

Pacius, Frederik (1809–91), Finnish composer of German origin. A pupil of Spohr, an excellent violinist and a musician of considerable culture, Pacius was one of the dominating musical figures of nineteenth-century Finland.

Parmet (Pergament-Parmet), Simon (1897–1943), Finnish conductor. After studying in Petrograd, Helsinki and Berlin, he spent some years working in German opera houses. Later he went to America conducting in various parts of the country and remaining there until 1948, when he returned to Finland. His study of Sibelius's symphonies appeared in 1955.

Paul, Adolf (1863–1942), Finnish author. Born in Sweden, Paul moved to Finland as a child, though most of his adult life was spent in Germany. His novel *En bok om en människa* (1891) shows the influence of Strindberg, and includes a character alleged by some writers to portray some of Sibelius's traits. A second book, *The Ripper* (1892), was banned at the time on account of its supposedly erotic character. His plays include

King Christian II, to which Sibelius provided a score; most of his dramatic works are in German. His output also includes a certain amount of poetry. During his later years he was an admirer of the Nazis.

Procopé, Hjalmar (1868–1927), Finnish poet and dramatist. Influenced by the poets of the nineties, Procopé was a writer of considerable intellectual distinction and, like Gripenberg, a spokesman of the Swedish-speaking minority. He was an outspoken champion of the independence movement. His works include collections of poems and plays, including *Belshazzars gästabud* (1905), *Fädrans anda* (1909) and *Inspektor på Siltala* (1915).

Ringbom, Nils-Eric (1907–   ), Finnish musicologist and composer. After studies at Åbo and in France he worked as a critic. Since 1942 he has held the post of managing director of the Helsinki Orchestra. As a composer his work comprises three symphonies and a wind sextet, together with other chamber works. His critical writings include a history of Helsinki's orchestral life (1882–1932) and a study of Sibelius published in 1948.

Runeberg, Johan Ludvig (1804–77), Finnish poet. Generally regarded as one of the finest poets writing in the Swedish language during the nineteenth century. After studying at Åbo he was appointed lecturer in classical languages at Helsinki. His poetry is noted for its lyricism and dignity of feeling. His first original collection of lyrical verse was published in 1830, and his most important works include a number of epic poems like *Nadezhda* and *Kung Fjalar*, which followed during the forties. *FänrikStåls Sägner* (1848, 1860) is regarded as one of the classics of Swedish literature.

Rydberg, Abraham Viktor (1828–95), Swedish poet, philosopher and historian. His first lyrical poems date from the sixties. His work includes a translation of *Faust*, a number of historical novels, several studies of German and Scandinavian mythology as well as a quantity of poetry. Among his most famous poems is the cantata written for the quatercentenary celebrations of Upsala University in 1877. In his last years he was professor of the history of art and aesthetics at Stockholm University.

Schnéevoigt, Georg (1872–1947), Finnish conductor. Studied at Helsinki and Leipzig, becoming a pupil of Fuchs in Vienna. For some years he was a cellist in the Helsinki Orchestra, and taught that instrument at the conservatoire. In 1901 he conducted at Riga and succeeded Weingartner in a Munich appointment. From 1914 to 1924 he was conductor of the Stockholm *Konsertförenings Orkester,* and founded the Oslo Philharmonic. He conducted in Oslo and Los Angeles on numerous occasions before succeeding Kajanus in Helsinki. He conducted the Finnish National Orchestra (as it was then called) on a visit to this country in 1934, when he recorded the sixth symphony of Sibelius.

Sibelius, Christian (1869–1922), Sibelius's brother. A fine cellist, Christian took part in public concerts with some success as a youngster. He studied medicine in Helsinki as well as music, and completed his medical studies in 1897, when he gained a doctorate. He was in charge of Lappvikens Mental Hospital from 1904 until his death, and was professor of psychiatry there.

Snellman, Johan Vilhelm (1806–81), Finnish writer, statesman and philosopher, who played an important part in Finnish national life during the nineteenth century.

Stagnelius, Erik Johan (1793–1823), Swedish poet and author whose reputation soared after his early death. His works include an epic poem, *Vladimir den Store* (1817), and a collection of poems, *Liljor i Saron*, together with a tragedy, *Bachanterna* (1823).

Stenhammar, Wilhelm (1871–1927), Swedish composer. A great admirer of both Sibelius and Nielsen, Stenhammar was undoubtedly the finest Swedish composer of his time. His output includes two symphonies, two piano concertos and six quartets. He was an enthusiastic conductor and directed performances of Sibelius's works in *Göteborgs Konsertförening*. The sixth symphony is dedicated to him.

Tavaststjerna, Karl August (1860–98), Finnish author and poet. His first collection of poetry appeared in 1883, *För morgonbris*, which already showed an independence of such models as Runeberg and Topelius. Tavaststjerna travelled widely and was cosmopolitan in outlook. Despite the cool reception of his work in Finland he was an outspoken patriot, and must be reckoned among the leading patriotic writers of the latter part of the century.

Topelius, Zacharius (1818–98), Finnish romantic poet. For many years he was editor of a Helsinki newspaper, and later became professor of history in Helsinki University. His most important prose work, *Fältskärns berätelser*, strove to foster a sense of national self-consciousness, and the novels of Walter Scott were the model on which he built. In later years he wrote mostly stories and poems for children.

Vecsey, Franz (1893–1935), Hungarian violinist. A pupil of Hubay and Joachim, Vecsey made his début internationally at the tender age of ten

(1903) and was regarded as one of the greatest masters of his instrument during the early decades of the present century. Although the first performances of both the original and revised versions of the Sibelius concerto were given by lesser-known players, Viktor Novaček and Karl Hallir respectively, the work is in fact dedicated to Vecsey, whom Sibelius heard when the violinist was still a child.

Wecksell, Josef Julius (1838–1907), Finnish poet. He is noted for his lyrics, many of which reflect the influence of Heine, and for his play *Daniel Hjort*, one of the key dramatic works written in Swedish before Strindberg.

Wegelius, Martin (1846–1906), Finnish composer, pupil of Faltin. Wegelius was active in Helsinki both as conductor and critic. He founded the Helsinki Music Institute and became its first director. His work includes a choral piece, *Julnatten*, an overture to *Daniel Hjort* and a setting of Runeberg's cantata (1878). An influential teacher, he was also the author of a history of Western music.

Wenneberg, Gunnar (1817–1901), Swedish composer and poet associated largely with the *Gluntarne*, songs and poems of student life in Upsala.

Wood, Ralph Walter (1902–   ), English composer and writer on music. A pupil of Howells, his work includes two symphonies, three quartets, a piano concerto and incidental music to Shakespeare's *Tempest*. He has written valuable studies of Tchaikovsky and Sibelius in symposiums edited by Gerald Abraham.

APPENDIX D

BIBLIOGRAPHY

Abraham, Gerald (ed.), 'Sibelius: a Symposium'. (London, 1947, 1952.)
Altmann, W., 'Jean Sibelius'. (*Allgemeine Musikzeitung*, Berlin, 1940.)
Andersson, Otto, 'Jean Sibelius'. (*Tidning för musik*, Helsinki, 1916.)
—— 'Jean Sibelius i Amerika'. (Åbo, 1955.)
—— 'Jean Sibelius och Svenska teatern'. (Åbo, 1956.)
——, 'När Jean Sibelius erhöll statsstipendium'. (*Hufvudstadsbladet*, Helsinki, 3 Jan. 1957.)
——, 'Sibelius och Kajanus som konkurrenter'. (*Hufvudstadsbladet*, Helsinki, 8 Dec. 1956.)
Arnold, Elliot, 'Finlandia: the Story of Sibelius'. (New York, 1941, 1951.)

Bantock, Granville, 'Jean Sibelius'. (*Monthly Musical Record*, London, Dec. 1935.
Beecham, Thomas, 'Sibelius, the Craftsman'. (*Living Age*, London, Feb. 1939.)
Bennet, Rodney, 'Song-writers of the Day: III—Jean Sibelius'. (*The Music Teacher*, London, Vol. V, No. 8, 1926.)
Blom, Eric, 'Sibelius'. (Cobbett's *Cyclopedic Survey of Chamber Music.*) (See also Abraham.)
Brodin, Gereon, 'Jean Sibelius' livsverk'. (*Vår Sång*, Stockholm, Vol. XIII, 1940.)

Cardus, Neville, 'Sibelius'. (*Ten Composers*, London, 1945.)
Cherniavsky, David, 'The Use of Germ Motives by Sibelius'. (*Music & Letters*, Vol. XXIII, London, 1942.)
——, 'Two Unpublished Tone-poems by Sibelius'. (*Musical Times*, 1949, p. 272.)
——, 'Sibelius's Tempo Corrections'. (*Music & Letters*, Vol. XXXI, 1950, p. 53.)
——, 'Sibelius and Finland'. (*Musical Times*, 1950.) (See also Abraham.)
Collins, Stuart, 'Germ Motives and Guff'. (*Music Review*, Vol. 23, 1962.)

Davie, Cedric Thorpe, 'Sibelius's Piano Sonatinas'. (*Tempo*, London, March 1945.)
Diktonius, Elmer, 'Opus 12, Musik'. (Helsinki, 1933.)
Downes, Olin, 'Sibelius the Symphonist'. (New York, 1956.)
Dyson, George, 'Sibelius'. (*Musical Times*, 1936, p. 987.)

Ekman, Karl, 'Jean, Sibelius: en Konstnärs liv och personlighet'. (Helsinki, 1935, 1936, 1956, 1959.)
Translated as 'J. S.: his Life and Personality'. (London, 1936; New York, 1938, 1946.)
Elliott, J. H., 'Jean Sibelius: a modern enigma'. (*The Chesterian*, London, Vol. XII, No. 92.)
——, 'The Sixth Symphony of Sibelius'. (*Music & Letters*, London, Vol. XVII, No. 3, July 1936.)

Flodin, Karl, 'Finska Musiker'. (Helsinki, 1900.)
Fougstedt, Nils-Erik, 'Sibelius' tonsättningar till Rydbergs texter'. (*Musikvärlden*, Stockholm, Vol. X, 1945, p. 16.)
Friederich, J., 'Wegbereiter seiner Nation'. (*Die Musik*, Berlin, Vol. XXVIII, 1935.)
Frosterus, Sigurd, 'Stålåldernas janusansikte och andra essäer. (Helsinki, 1935.)
Funtek, L., 'Jean Sibelius' konstnärskap'. (*Musikern*, Stockholm, Vol. XVIII, 1925.)
Furuhjelm, Erik, 'Jean Sibelius, hans tondiktning och drag ur hans liv'. (Borgå, 1916.)
Translated into Finnish by Leevi Madetoja. (Porvoo, 1916.)
——, 'Jean Sibelius'. (*Ord och Bild*, Vol. XXIII, Stockholm, 1914.)

Gilie, G., 'Jean Sibelius som orkesterdirigent'. (*Musikern*, Stockholm, 1925.)
Goddard, Scott, 'Sibelius's Second Symphony'. (*Music & Letters*, London, April 1931.)
Göhler, G., 'Jean Sibeliuksen varhaisemmat orkesterisävellykset' ('The Earlier Orchestral Compositions of Sibelius'). (*Kalevalaseuran vuosikirja*, Helsinki, 1926.)
Gray, Cecil, 'Sibelius'. (London, 1931, 1934, 1945.)
——, 'Sibelius: the Symphonies'. (London, 1935.)
——, 'Sibelius, or Music and the Future'. (*The Nation and Athenaeum*, Dec. 24, 1927.)

Gray, Cecil, Musical Chairs. (London, 1948, pp. 255–60.)
Gregory, R., 'Sibelius and the Kalevala'. (*Monthly Musical Record*, Vol. LXXXI, 1951.)
Gripenberg, B., 'Till Jean Sibelius på 70-årsdagen'. (Helsinki, 1935.)

Haapanen, T., 'Den nationella betydelsen av Jean Sibelius' konst'. (*Musikern*, Stockholm, 1925.)
——, 'Piirteitä Jean Sibeliuksen elämästä ja taiteesta' ('Aspects of Sibelius's Life and Art'). (Helsinki, 1925.)
——, 'Jean Sibelius, elämä ja merkitys' ('Sibelius: his Life and Importance'). (*Kulttuurin saavutuksia*, Helsinki, 1946.)
Hannikainen, I., 'Hieman Sibeliuksen pianosävellyksistä'. (*Suomen musiikkilehti*, Helsinki, 1935.)
——, 'Sibelius and the Development of Finnish Music'. (London, 1948.)
Hauch, G., 'Jean Sibelius'. (Copenhagen, 1915.)
Helasvuo, V., 'Sibelius and the Music of Finland'. (Helsinki, 1952, 1957.)
Hemming, Aare, 'Jean Sibeliuksen Lemminkäis-sarjan kaksi osaa Lemminkäinen ja Saaren neidot sekä Lemminkäinen Tuonelassa: Muotoja teema-analyysiä' ('Two Parts of Sibelius's *Lemminkäinen* Suite (Nos. 1 and 3): formal and thematic analysis'). (Helsinki University, 1956.)[1]
Herbage, Julian, 'Jean Sibelius'. (*The Symphony*, ed. Ralph Hill, London, 1949.)
Hill, W., 'Some Aspects of Form in the Symphonies of Sibelius'. (*Music Review*, Vol. X, 1949.)

Ingman, O., 'Jean Sibelius: Voces Intimae'. (Helsinki University, 1958.)[1]

Jacobs, R. L., 'Sibelius' Lemminkainen and the Maidens of Sari'. (*Musie Review*, Vol. XXIV, 1963.)
Jalas, Jussi, 'Valse triste och musiken till "Kuolema"'. (*Musikvärlden*, Stockholm, May 1948.)
Jalas, Margareta, 'Jean Sibelius: kuvateos—in pictures'. (Helsinki, 1952, 1958.)
Jeanson, Gunnar, 'Jean Sibelius och Carl Nielsen'. (*Nordens kalendar*, Göteborg, 1934.)
Johnson, Harold, 'Jean Sibelius'. (New York, 1959, London, 1960.)

---

[1] These are both licentiate theses in the library of Helsinki University.

Johnson, Harold, 'Jean Sibeliuksen "Andante lirico"'. (*Helsingin Sanomat*, June 15, 1958.)

——, 'Jean Sibeliuksen "Lemminkäis-sarja"'. (*Helsingin Sanomat*, May 19, 1957.)

——, 'Jean Sibeliuksen "Työkansan marssi"'. (*Helsingin Sanomat*, July 5, 1958.)

——, 'Sibelius fjärde symfoni—en stråkkvartett?' (*Nya Pressen*, June 7, 1958.)

Kajanus, Robert, 'Sibelius—siaren'. (*Musikern*, Stockholm, 1925.)

Konow, Walter von, 'Muistoja Jean Sibeliuksen poikavuosilta'. (*Aulos*, Helsinki, 1925.)

——, 'Janne'. (*Veckans Krönika*, Dec. 4, 1915.)

Kotilainen, O., 'Mestarin muokattavana'. (*Aulos*, Helsinki, 1925.)

Krohn Ilmari, 'Der Formenbau in den Symphonien von Jean Sibelius'. (Helsinki, 1942.)

——, 'Der Stimmungsgehalt in den Symphonien von Jean Sibelius'. (In two vols.) (Helsinki, 1945, 1946.)

Lambert, Constant, 'Music, Ho! A study of music in decline'. (Chapter entitled 'Sibelius and the Integration of Form'.) (London, 1934.)

Layton, Robert, 'Sibelius: the early years'. (*Proceedings of the Royal Music Association*, 1964–5.)

Leibowitz, René, 'Jean Sibelius, le plus mauvais compositeur du monde'. (Liège, 1955.)

Levas, Santeri, 'Jean Sibelius ja hänen Ainolansa'. (Helsinki, 1945, 1955.)

——, 'Nuori Sibelius' ('The Young Sibelius'). (Porvoo, 1957.)

——, 'Sibelius, Muistelmia suuresta ihmisestä. Järvenpään mestari'. (Porvoo, 1960.)

Lyla, W., 'The "Nationalism" of Jean Sibelius'. (*Musical Quarterly*, New York, 1927.)

Madetoja, Leevi, 'Jean Sibelius oppetajana'. (*Aulos*, Helsinki, 1925.)

Marvia, Einari, 'Jean Sibeliuksen musikaalinen sukuperintö'. (*Uusi Musiikkilehti*, No. 9, Helsinki, 1955, pp. 49–81.)

Mellers, Wilfred, 'Sibelius and the Modern Mind'. (*Music Survey*, Vol. I, No. 6, pp. 177–183.)

——, 'Sibelius at Ninety: A Revaluation'. (*Listener*, Dec. 1955.)

Meyer, Alfred 'Sibelius, Symphonist'. (*Musical Quarterly*, New York, 1936.)

Newmarch, Rosa, 'Jean Sibelius: A Finnish Composer'. (Leipzig, 1906.)
—, 'Jean Sibelius: A Short History of a Long Friendship'. (Boston, 1939; London, 1945.)
Niemann, Walter, 'Jean Sibelius'. (Leipzig, 1917.)
Nyblom, C G., 'Jean Sibelius'. (Stockholm, 1916.)
Nyssönen, J., 'Jean Sibelius'. (Budapest, 1936.) (In collaboration with I. Schiffer.)

Ottelin, O., 'Sibelius' Symfonier som personliga dokument och som nationell skatt'. (*Studiekamraten,* Vol. XXVII, Stockholm, 1945.)
—, 'Sibelius och naturen'. (*Studiekamraten,* Vol. XXII, Stockholm, 1940.)
—, 'Tolv nordiska porträtt'. (Stockholm, 1945.)

Pajanne, Martti, 'Muusikkojen muistelmia mestarista orkesterinjohtajana'. (*Uusi Musiikkilehti,* No. 9, Helsinki, 1955.)
Parmet, Simon, 'Sibelius Symfonier'. (Helsinki, 1955.) Translated as 'The Symphonies of Sibelius'. (London, 1959.)
—, 'Ur en essä om interpretationen av Sibelius' musik'. (*Nya Argus,* Helsinki, No. 10, 1949.)
Pfaler, S. von, 'Sånger av Sibelius till ord av Runeberg'. (*Finsk tidskrift,* Åbo, 1945.)
Pirsch, G., 'Jean Sibelius'. (Gilly-Charleroi, 1944.)
Paul, Adolf, 'När Sibelius dirigerade'. (*Profiler,* Stockholm, 1937.)
—, 'Mein Freund Sibelius'. (*Volkischer Beobachter,* Berlin, Jan. 27, 1938.)

Ranta, J., 'Jean Sibeliuksen "Kullervo-symfonian" esitys v. 1892: vanhan miehen muistelmia' ('The Performance of Sibelius's Kullervo Symphony in 1892: A memoir'). (*Musiikkitieto,* Helsinki, 1933, p. 140.)
Ranta, Sulho. 'Jean Sibelius'. (*Suomen säveltäjiä* (Finnish Composers), Porvoo, 1945.)
—, 'Sibeliuksen musiikin esittelyä'. (*Kulttuurin saavutuksia,* Helsinki, 1946.)
Ringbom Nils-Eric, 'Litteraturen om Jean Sibelius'. (*Svensk Tidskrift för Musikforskning,* Stockholm, 1942.)
—, 'Sibelius och impressionismen'. (*Finsk Tidskrift,* Åbo, 1948.)
—, 'Sibelius'. (Stockholm, 1948.) (Translated Oklahoma, 1954.)
—, 'Sibelius' utvecklingsskeden'. (*Musikrevy,* Stockholm, 1950.)

Ringbom, Nils-Eric, 'De två versionerna av Sibelius' tondikt "En Saga"'. (Åbo, 1956.)

Roiha Eino, 'Die Symphonien von Jean Sibelius: Eine formanalytische Studie'. (Jyväskylä, 1941.)

Rosas, John, 'Sibelius' musik till skådespelet Ödlan'. Suomen Musiikin Vuosikirja, 1960–1.)

—, 'Otryckta Kammarmusikverk av Jean Sibelius'. (Åbo, 1961.)

Rosenfeld, Paul, 'Sibelius'. (Musical Portraits, London, 1922.)

Sandberg, Börje, 'Jean Sibelius'. (Helsinki, 1940.)

Schiffer, I., See under Nyssönen.

Schouwman, H., 'Sibelius'. (Antwerp, 1949.)

Similä, M., 'Sibeliana'. (Helsinki, 1945.)

Simpson, Robert, 'Sibelius and Nielsen'. (B.B.C., 1965.)

Solanterä, Lauri, 'The Works of Jean Sibelius'. (Helsinki, 1955.)

—, 'Sibelius'. (Facsimiles of manuscripts: notes by Eino Roiha.) (Helsinki, 1945.)

Tanzberger, E., 'Jean Sibelius'. (Wiesbaden, 1962.)

—, 'Die symphonischen Dichtungen von Jean Sibelius'. (Würzburg, 1943.)

—, 'Jean Sibelius als Symphoniker'. (*Gesellschaft für Musikforschung, Kongressbericht,* Lüneburg, 1950.)

Tawaststjerna, Erik, 'The Pianoforte Compositions of Jean Sibelius'. (Helsinki, 1957.)

—, 'Ton och Tolkning'. (Swedish translation of above, with additional chapters.) (Helsinki, 1957.)

Törnblom, Folke, 'Sibelius och Kalevala'. (*Vår Sång,* Stockholm, 1942.)

Törne, Bengt von, 'Sibelius: A Close-Up'. (London, Boston, 1937.)

—, 'Sibelius, i närbild och samtal'. (Helsinki, 1945, 1955).

—, 'Sibelius som människa och konstnär'. (*Nordisk Tidskrift,* Stockholm, 1946.)

Tovey, Donald, 'Analyses of works by Sibelius'. (*Essays in Musical Analysis,* Vol. II (London, 1935), Vol. III (1936) and Vol. VI (1939).)

Truscott, Harold, 'A Sibelian Fallacy'. (*The Chesterian,* London, Vol. XXXII, 1957.)

—, 'The Greatness of Sibelius'. (*Listener,* 1963.)

—, 'Sibelius'. (*The Symphony.* Ed. Robert Simpson.) (Penguin Books, London, 1965.)

Vainio, A., 'Sibeliuksen kehitys orkesterisäveltäjäksi '('Sibelius's Development as an orchestral composer'). (*Suomalainen Suomi*, Helsinki, 1946.)
Väisänen, A. O., 'Sibelius ja kansanmusiikki'. ('Sibelius and Folk-Music'). (*Kalevalaseuran vuosikirja*, Helsinki, Vol. XVI, 1936.)
——, 'Kalevala ja säveltaide' ('The Kalevala and Music'). (*Kalevalaseuran vuosikirja*, Helsinki, Vols. XXVII–XXVIII, 1947–8.)
——, 'Kanteletarta sävellettynä' ('Compositions to the Kantelar'). (*Kalevalaseuran vuosikirja*, Vol. XXXI, 1951.)
——, 'Sibeliuksen Kullervo-sinfonian valta-aiheista' ('On the themes of Sibelius's Kullervo symphony'). (*Kalevalaseuran vuosikirja*, Vol. XXXIII, 1953.)
——, 'Sibelius om sina Kalevala-kompositioner'. (*Musikern*, Stockholm, 1925.)
Vestdijk, Simon, 'De symfonieën van Jean Sibelius'. (Amsterdam, 1962.)
Vitt, B., 'Jean Sibelius'. (*Allgemeine Musikzeitung*, Berlin, 1935.)
Voipo, Anni, 'Sibelius as his wife sees him'. (*New York Times*, Jan. 28, 1940.)
Vuolijoki, S., 'Hämettä ja hämäläisiä' ('Sibelius as a conductor'). (Helsinki, 1945, pp. 43–7.)

Witeschnik, A., 'Jean Sibelius, "der getreue Eckart"'. (Vienna, 1940.)
Wood, Ralph W., 'Sibelius's Use of Percussion'. (*Music & Letters*, London, Vol. XXIII, 1942.)
(See also Abraham.)

INDEX